T0103883

Implementing the Stakeholder based Goal-Question-Metric (GQM) Measurement Model for Software Projects

Dr. Prashanth Harish Southekal

Order this book online at www.trafford.com
or email orders@trafford.com

Most Trafford titles are also available at major online book retailers.

© Copyright 2014 Dr. Prashanth Harish Southekal.
All rights reserved. No part of this publication may be reproduced, stored in a retrieval
system, or transmitted, in any form or by any means, electronic, mechanical, photocopying,
recording, or otherwise, without the written prior permission of the author.

Printed in the United States of America.

ISBN: 978-1-4907-4009-6 (sc)
ISBN: 978-1-4907-4008-9 (e)

Because of the dynamic nature of the Internet, any web addresses or links contained in
this book may have changed since publication and may no longer be valid. The views
expressed in this work are solely those of the author and do not necessarily reflect the
views of the publisher, and the publisher hereby disclaims any responsibility for them.

Any people depicted in stock imagery provided by Thinkstock are models,
and such images are being used for illustrative purposes only.
Certain stock imagery © Thinkstock.

Trafford rev. 06/24/2014

 www.trafford.com

North America & international
toll-free: 1 888 232 4444 (USA & Canada)
fax: 812 355 4082

Contents

Acknowledgements ix

List of Key Acronyms and Abbreviations xi

Abstract xiii

Chapter 1   Introduction 1

1.1 Introduction 1

1.2 The Research Theme 2

    1.2.1 Varied value propositions of the stakeholders. 3

    1.2.2 Inherent challenges in software projects. 3

    1.2.3 Lack of proven measures. 6

1.3 The Research Problem and Questions 7

1.4 Assumptions, Limitations and Delimitations in this research 9

1.5 Research Flow 10

1.6 Conclusion 12

Chapter 2   Literature Review 13

2.1 Introduction 13

2.2 Basics of Measurement Theory 13

2.3 Addressing the Research Questions 20

    2.3.1 Definition of a Software Project 21

    2.3.2 Software Project Success Criteria 25

    2.3.3. Overview of Measurement frameworks. 29

    2.3.4 Validation of Measurement Models 38

    2.3.5 Current Measurement Models 41

2.4 Conclusion 45

**Chapter 3   Research Approach – The Paradigm,
             Design and Methodology** **47**

3.1 Introduction 47

3.2 Research Paradigm 48

3.3 Research Design 51

3.4 Research Methodology 53

    3.4.1: Step 1- Identification of the Measurement Framework 54

    3.4.2 Step 2: Derivation of the Measurement Model 56

    3.4.3 Step 3: Derivation of the Validation Criteria 71

    3.4.4 Step 4: Validation 78

    3.4.4.1 Theoretical Validation 78

    3.4.4.2 Empirical Validation 78

3.5 Empirical Validation with Case studies 79

3.6 Empirical Validation with Survey 81

    3.6.1 Descriptive Statistics 83

    3.6.2 Inferential Statistics 85

3.7 Reliability of Empirical Validation 94

3.8 Conclusion 97

Chapter 4   Analysis of Research Results **98**

4.1 Introduction 98

4.2 Analysis of Theoretical Validation 98

    4.2.1 Analysis of Seven Theoretical Validation Criteria 99

    4.2.2 Analysis of Kaner-Bond Questionnaire 104

4.3 Analysis of Empirical Validation 108

    4.3.1 Analysis of the Case Study 108

    4.3.1.1 Overview of the Case Study 108

    4.3.1.2 Ensuring Reliability in the Case Study 110

    4.3.1.3 Data Collection 112

    4.3.1.4 Case Study 2: Uncontrolled Instance 116

    4.3.2 Analysis of Survey Results 119

    4.3.2.1 Overview of the Survey 119

    4.3.2.2 Data Collection in the Survey: Descriptive Statistics 119

    4.3.2.3 Analysis of Survey: Inferential Statistics 125

4.3.3.4 Ensuring Reliability in the Survey 135

4.3.3.5 Debate on having LOC in the Measurement Model 137

4.3.3.6 Other Feedback in the Survey 140

4.4 Conclusion 141

Chapter 5   Discussion on Research Results **142**

5.1 Introduction... 142

5.2 Results of Theoretical Validation.. 142

5.3 Results of Empirical Validation 145

5.3.1 Results of Case Studies 145

5.3.2 Results of the Survey 151

5.4 Contribution to Body of Knowledge (BoK)........................ 153

5.5 Conclusion 155

Chapter 6   Conclusion **156**

6.1 Introduction... 156

6.2 Assumptions in this Research... 156

6.3 Limitations of this Research 157

6.4 Future Research... 160

6.5 Conclusion 162

Appendix 1 204 Questions to the Project Stakeholders **165**

Appendix 2 The Eight Measures in the Measurement Model...... **180**

Appendix 3 Definition of the 14 Validation Criteria **198**

Appendix 4 Survey Questionnaire..**203**

References...**205**

Acknowledgements

This book is an adaption of my PhD thesis and there are many people who have positively impacted my "PhD project". I would like to thank them for their role in the completion of this doctoral thesis on "Formulation and Validation of a Generic and Objective Goal-Question-Metric (GQM) Based Measurement Model for Software Projects". Pursuing the PhD program was a unique learning and collaborative experience and it has definitely been one of my best "investments" till date.

I thank my PhD supervisors - Dr Ginger Levin and Dr Darren Dalcher, who have supported me with their knowledge, rigor and patience whilst providing me the space to experiment and work according to my style and convenience. While I had two formal advisors in Dr Levin and Dr Dalcher, I am extremely grateful to Professor Guenther Ruhe, Professor — Department of Computer Science and Electrical Engineering at the University of Calgary (UoC), Canada who was my location mentor in Calgary. I am also grateful to reviewers from IEEE ESEM, IEEE ICSSP and IEEE ICCI conferences for their feedback while accepting my papers pertaining to this research thesis.

In the entire research period, I had numerous discussions with top researchers and industry practitioners who were instrumental in giving a better shape to this research. The list includes Capers Jones (Software Productivity Council, US), Professor Yingxu Wang (University of Calgary, Canada), Dr Peter Jackson (Cornell University, US), Dr KC Shashidhar (Max Planck Institute, Germany), Tom Gilb (Result Planning Limited, Norway), Professor Dev Priya Soni (JIIT, India), Robert

Ferguson (SEI), Professor PP Iyer (Indian Institute of Science, India), Dr. Stephane Vaucher (Metrics Specialist, Benchmark Consulting, Canada), Michael Roomey (Master Black Belt, General Electric, US), Ray Stratton (President, Management Technologies, US), and Abhay Shetty (Project Manager, SAP AG, India).

I am extremely grateful to my former employers Accenture Canada and SAP AG for providing me a conducive and stimulating work atmosphere for research. I am also grateful to ATB Financial, Canada, for giving me an opportunity to implement this research in the Core SAP banking implementation program. I am also thankful to my parents, my in-laws, and my sister and her family for all their help, blessings and wishes. Finally, I owe my loving thanks to my wife Shruthi who has supported and encouraged me in all my pursuits and my two wonderful kids Pranathi "Panna" and Prathik "Heera".

Dr. Prashanth Harish Southekal
Calgary, AB, Canada
May 2014.

List of Key Acronyms and Abbreviations

- AC – Actual Cost
- BSC – Balanced Scorecard
- CA – Control Account
- COQ – Cost of Quality
- COTS – Commercial-Off-The-Shelf
- CMMI - Capability Maturity Model Integration
- Cpk – Sigma Level
- CPI – Cost Performance Index
- CV – Cost Variance
- DD – Defect Density
- DPMO - Defects Per Million Opportunities
- DRE – Defect Removal Efficiency
- ESE – Empirical Software Engineering
- EVM – Earned Value Management
- FP – Function Point
- GQM – Goal Question Metric
- ISO - International Organization for Standardization
- IT - Information Technology
- JAD – Joint Application Development
- KPI - Key Performance Indicator
- (K)LOC – (Kilo) Lines of Code
- OBS – Organizational Breakdown Structure
- PCA – Paired Comparison Analysis
- PMB – Performance Measurement Baseline
- PMBOK – Project Management Body of Knowledge
- PMI - Project Management Institute
- PSM – Practical Software Measurement

- RBS – Requirement Breakdown Structure
- ROI - Return on Investment
- SAAS – Software As A Service
- SDLC – Software Development Lifecycle
- SEI – Software Engineering Institute
- SPI – Schedule Performance Index
- SPI - Software Process Improvement
- SRS - Software Requirement Specification
- SS – Sample size
- SV – Schedule Variance
- TCO - Total Cost of Ownership
- V(G) – McCabe's Cyclomatic Complexity
- VOC – Voice of the Customer
- VOP – Voice of the Process
- WBS – Work Breakdown Structure

Abstract

Software projects are often strategic business transformation initiatives within the organization. Any failure in its implementation is often devastating to the organization. While software projects are inherently complex in delivery, one of the approaches for successful project delivery is formulating an objective stakeholder driven measurement model encompassing their key value propositions so that decision makers are well informed on the project progress. Based on the Goal-Question-Metric (GQM) framework, this research derived a generic, objective and stakeholder driven measurement model using six steps for hybrid COTS (Commercial off-the-shelf) and bespoke types of software projects. The measurement model derived includes eight measures related to five project attributes. The eight measures are Function Points (FPs), Lines of Code (LOC), McCabe's Cyclomatic Complexity (VG), Cost Performance Index (CPI), Schedule Performance Index (SPI), Sigma level (Cpk), Defect Density (DD) and Defect Removal Efficiency (DRE) and the five project attributes are size, complexity, schedule, cost and quality. The project status report with these eight measures resting on a set of assumptions, limitations and delimitations is meant to be a succinct summary capturing critical information most relevant to the project stake holders with scope to add more measures depending on the unique project circumstances and context.

According to software metrics researchers, a robust measurement model is the one that is not only scientifically derived and but is also validated —theoretically and empirically. On theoretical validation of the measurement model, seven criteria from measurement theory were applied on the measures. The theoretical validation on each measure not only characterizes the property it claims to measure but also minimize the chances of failure encountered during the implementation by addressing exceptions. In addition, the ten questions of Cem Kaner and Walter Bond were also applied on the measurement model for a holistic approach.

Though theoretical validation is getting a great deal of attention from researchers, industry practitioners still rely on the empirical evidence of a measure's utility. Hence the measurement model was empirically validated using mixed research model with case studies (controlled and uncontrolled) and survey (Ordinal Likert response scale). The measurement model was first empirically validated (Qualitative research) by implementing it in a real world software project (a hybrid COTS project in a controlled setting) and the results showed that the measurement model was useful to bring the project for its successful completion. Also another project (a bespoke project in an uncontrolled setting) which used the measurement model partially was challenged as the stakeholders did not have accurate and complete information of the project status. To bring more depth to the empirical validation, survey questionnaire (Quantitative research) was then implemented and responses collected from 123 industry practitioners from 32 countries reflecting close to 2000 years of their software project experience. Inferential statistical analysis on the survey responses showed that eight measures can indeed be used to predict the project outcome and cater to the stakeholder value propositions. The survey and the two case studies demonstrated that the measurement model (based on a set of assumptions, limitations and delimitations) can be used to provide critical information at the right time for proactive decision making in hybrid COTS and bespoke types of software projects.

Good software project management demands only a handful of validated and objective measures which can be easily and quickly applied to gauge the health of the project holistically and to complete the project successfully. The proposed measurement model encompasses the key value propositions of the project stakeholders with a set of eight measures.

List of Figures

Figure 1: Research Process 11

Figure 2: Software Measurement Process 14

Figure 3: Measurement Model 15

Figure 4: Mathematical description of Measurement Construct 20

Figure 5: Comparison of the three types of software projects 24

Figure 6: D&M IS Success Model 28

Figure 7: Software Project Success Criteria 29

Figure 8: Chronology of Measurement Frameworks 30

Figure 9: Balanced Scorecard 32

Figure 10: PSM Measurement Process Model 34

Figure 11: GQM Model 36

Figure 12: Structural Model of Measurement 40

Figure 13: Citation Network 41

Figure 14: Building Blocks of Research 48

Figure 15: IS Research Framework 49

Figure 16: Research Design 53

Figure 17: GMFs Validation with software industry practitioners 55

Figure 18: Pruning the Baseline Questions 61

Figure 19: The Six Steps in GQM 70

Figure 20: Stakeholder driven GQM framework 71

Figure 22: The Hypothesis Framework 94

Figure 23: Survey Analysis Flowchart 96

Figure 24: Four Step "Hybrid" RUP Methodology 111

Figure 25: McCabe's Output from Eclipse plug-in 113

Figure 26: Measurement Model in the Case Study 116

Figure 27: Profile of the Survey Respondents 120

Figure 28: Product Measures i.e. FP, LOC and V(G) 121

Figure 29: EVM Measures i.e. SPI and CPI..122

Figure 30: Quality Measures i.e. Cpk, DD and DRE............................122

Figure 31: Response for the Overall Measure i.e. Om........................123

Figure 32: NPS Statistics in Percentages 126

Figure 33: Correlation between the Means of 8 Measures and Om.....128

Figure 34: Correlation Values for Survey Validity................................136

Figure 35: Comparison of the Eight Measures.......................................147

Figure 36: NPS Efficiency...151

Figure A: McCabe Complexity Example..186

Figure B: Building blocks of EVM 190

Figure C: Measurement Mapping...201

List of Tables

Table 1:   Information Level in Measurement Scales.............................. 18
Table 2:   Expectations of the Project Stakeholders 26
Table 3:   Dalcher's definition of software project success................... 27
Table 4:   Comparison of the three GMFs. 38
Table 5:   Comparison of Measurement Models 43
Table 6:   Research Paradigm elements... 50
Table 7:   Strengths and Weakness of Qualitative and
           Quantitative Methods.. 52
Table 8:   Comparison of goal-oriented measurement
           frameworks (GMF) 54
Table 9:   Project Stakeholder Value Propositions 57
Table 10: Baseline Question Formulation 59
Table 11: Summarized Data from
           Paired Comparison Analysis (PCA) 63
Table 12: Application of the five criteria on the eight measures........ 69
Table 13: List of all 47 validation criteria 72
Table 14: Top Six Software Metrics Validation Criteria Papers 73
Table 15: List of 28 validation criteria.. 73
Table 16: List of 17 Validation Criteria.. 76
Table 17: List of Final 14 Validation Criteria..................................77
Table 18: Empirical Validation Criteria.. 79
Table 19: Format for Analyzing Pearson's correlation co-efficient..... 87
Table 20: Null Hypothesis Statements for Correlation 87
Table 21: Format for the application of KW test on the three
           stakeholder groups 92
Table 22: Scale Type Property.. 99
Table 23: Granularity of Measures 100
Table 24: Representation Condition (RC) Validity............................ 101

Table 25: Unit Validity 101
Table 26: Protocol Validity 102
Table 27: Appropriate continuity 102
Table 28: Dimensional Consistency 103
Table 29: Attributes of the Measures 104
Table 30: Natural Scales of the Measures 105
Table 31: Earning Rules for SPI and CPI 115
Table 32: Similarities between Two Case Studies 117
Table 33: Frequency of Survey Responses 121
Table 34: Skewness Values of Survey Responses 123
Table 35: Kurtosis Values of Survey Responses 124
Table 36: Central tendency summarized by Median 124
Table 37: Variability summarized by Range and IQR 125
Table 38: NPS efficiency based on stakeholder groups............ 127
Table 39: t-values.. 128
Table 40: p-values.. 129
Table 41: Regression summary 129
Table 42: Regression Analysis Hypothesis 131
Table 43: Relationship between Similar Constructs 132
Table 44: p-values and hypothesis inference............................ 134
Table 45: Index of Variation 137
Table 46: Analysis of LOC data based on Organization types........ 137
Table 47: Analysis of LOC data based on Stakeholder types.......... 138
Table 48: Analysis of LOC data based on Developer Skills 138
Table 49: Analysis of LOC and v (G) 139
Table 50: Summarized Theoretical Validation Criteria 143
Table 51: Validating Measures using the Ten Questions 144
Table 52: Measurement Data after the First Iteration 145
Table 53: Measurement Data after the Final Iteration 146
Table 54: Summary of Association Validation Criteria 152
Table A: Function Point Factors 184
Table B: Original McCabe values for Program complexity............ 187
Table C: Interpretations of Basic EVM Performance Measures
           [PMI, 2004] 192
Table D: Sigma Level V/s DPMO 194
Table E: DRE v/s Process Maturity 197

Chapter 1

Introduction

1.1 Introduction

In the recent years the landscape of software project management has undergone significant metamorphosis around the globe due to the increased need for cheaper-faster-better software. Software solutions are changing to be user centric, web centric, service oriented and implemented through new delivery models such as Software-As-A-Service (SaaS), Grid computing, Agile, Outsourcing et cetera. Software project management is no longer considered a technical endeavor; it has transformed itself into a multi-disciplinary business engagement, requiring alignment of business and IT strategies within an organization for enhanced employee productivity, higher degree of information accuracy, faster product launch to name a few. As software projects are invariably strategic initiatives in the organization, software project failure is often devastating. A reliable measurement model, which is the goal of this research thesis can inform the stakeholders on the project status and this can potentially prevent project issues such as schedule slips, cost overruns, and missing features to name a few.

This chapter is presented as follows. Section 1.2 gives the background behind this research and sets the tone for the remainder part of the thesis. The research problem statement and questions are formulated in section 1.3. Given that research will generally be based on assumptions, limitations and delimitations, section 1.4 covers this. Section 1.5 proposes the research flow based on Trochim's hour glass

1

model. Finally section 1.6 summarizes this chapter and sets the tone for the next chapter i.e. literature review.

1.2 The Research Theme

Metrology is one of the driving forces for the development and maturity of engineering disciplines including software engineering [Wang, 2003]. Research has shown that in successful software projects the primary control mechanism has been the measurement [Vierimaa et al, 2001]. Numerous researchers and organizations have emphasized the importance of measurement in software projects. John Reel includes "track progress" as one of the five essential factors for successfully managing a software project [Reel, 1999]. According to SL Pfleeger and Norman Fenton, "A robust measurement framework helps to take suitable corrective actions in the project at the right time" [Pfleeger et al, 2002]. Karl Wigers includes "Track project status openly and honestly" as one of the top 21 secrets of successful software project management [Weigers, 2002]. Larry Putnam says that software projects can be managed for success with progress indicators applied through metrics based management [Putnam, 2002]. According to Roger Pressman, the software project management activities should include measurement [Pressman, 2004]. Measurement is an important element in all the ten knowledge areas of the software engineering body of knowledge [SWEBOK, 2004]. Industry standards such as ISO 9000 and industry models like the Software Engineering Institute's (SEI) Capability Maturity Model Integrated (CMMI) recommend having measurement for successful delivery of software projects.

However metrics management is often the most complicated project management process as the stakeholders including the project manager generally cannot tell precisely where the project stands [Humphrey, 2005]. According to Christian and Ferns, a software project is often assumed to be unmeasurable [Christian and Ferns, 1995] and according to Norman Fenton much of the metrics programs in the industry is poorly motivated and executed [Fenton, 2006]. Industry averages show that only 20 percent of measurement programs implemented survive past the two-year mark [Dekkers and McQuaid, 2002]. In this backdrop, the **research area** concentrates on **deriving a reliable measurement model for software projects.** Though there are many reasons for not having reliable measurement models for software projects, three reasons frequently stand out and these three reasons are explained below.

1.2.1 Varied value propositions of the stakeholders.

Used as a general term, stakeholder can be defined as individual, groups or organizations that have an interest in the outcome of the project. Project stakeholders generally have varied level of interest, involvement and influence on the project and their goals vary and conflict reflecting different political and organizational interests. In addition, in most projects the expectations of the stakeholders are implicit and subjective and given the dynamic nature of software projects, getting reliable measurement data quickly to understand the project status is a huge challenge. Fundamentally meeting or exceeding stakeholder needs or expectations involves balancing the competing demands among [Smith, 2000]:

- Scope, schedule, cost and quality
- Stakeholders with differing needs and expectations
- Identified requirements (needs) and unidentified requirements (expectations)

The varied interests and changing needs of the stakeholders has primarily resulted in having measurement models (and project status reports) not completely catering to the value propositions of the stakeholders.

1.2.2 Inherent challenges in software projects.

By their nature software projects are generally dynamic; they tend to grow, change, and behave in ways it cannot always be predicted. They are usually governed by constraints which are multidimensional and abstract in nature and encompass making critical decisions at different

3

software development lifecycle (SDLC) phases. In this backdrop, leveraging the work of Frederick Brooks and Steve McConnell, Fairley observed that there are five key attributes that make the management software projects challenging [Fairley, 2009]. The five attributes are:

1. Complexity

Nearly all software projects exhibit some degree of complexity. Frederick Brooks, states that "Software entities are more complex than perhaps any other human construct. Many of the classical problems of developing software products derive from this essential complexity" [Brooks, 1995, pp 182]. According to Roger Sessions, the primary cause of software project failures is complexity [Sessions, 2010]. According to Remington and Oollack, there are four types of software project complexity and any software project will exhibit one or more types of complexity [Remington and Oollack, 2008]. They are:

i. **Structural Complexity**

This kind of complexity is normally found in large projects due to the difficulty in managing and keeping track of the huge number of different interconnected tasks and activities.

ii. **Technical/System complexity**

This type of complexity is found in projects which have technical or design problems associated with products that has never been produced before. This is also known as system complexity and encompasses three key dimensions [Xia and Lee, 2005]:

- Variety. It is the multiplicity of project elements such as number of sites or applications affected by the system implementation.
- Variability. This refers to changes in project elements such as changes in project goal and scope.
- Integration. This taps into coordination of various project elements.

iii. **Directional complexity**

Directional complexity is found in projects which are characterized by lack of clarity, unshared goals and goal paths, unclear meanings and hidden agendas amongst the project stakeholders. This kind of complexity stems from ambiguity related to multiple interpretations of goals and objectives.

iv. **Temporal complexity**

These projects are characterized by shifting environmental and strategic directions which are generally outside the direct control of the project team. This kind of complexity stems from uncertainty regarding system dependencies, external constraints, new/disruptive technologies, competition, government regulations et cetera.

2. Conformity

Essentially software must conform to exacting specifications in the representation of each part, in the interfaces to other internal parts, and in the connections to the environment in which it operates. The software must also conform to real-world constraints—pre-existing hardware, third party components, government regulations, data formats, and so on. A syntactic error can be detected by a compiler but a defect in the program logic, or a timing error, may be difficult to detect. Interfaces among software applications or modules must agree exactly in numbers and data types of parameters. Ultimately lack of conformity might not be discovered until late in a software project and resulting in unplanned allocation of resources eventually affecting the outcome of the project.

3. Changeability

Software generally provides most of the functionality in software-intensive systems. Because software is the most easily changed element in a software-intensive system, it is the most frequently changed element in the system. While the change impacts the complexity and conformity, it often results in undesired side effects in other areas of the system. Also the more successful the software application is, the more uses people will find for it, and the more it will be adapted beyond the domain for which it was originally intended.

4. Invisibility

The biggest difference between software and other kinds of engineering projects is that software is not physical or visible; it is an intangible entity. Due to the lack of visualization of the software product, customer i.e. the user cannot have any underlying sense of what is attainable and may ask for functions that are impossible to deliver. Their inability to visualize the boundaries creates indifference to what is possible and what is not and encourages the software users to change their minds more frequently [Gross, 2006] resulting in scope volatility and creep.

5. PeopleWare

According to Fairley, software projects are intellect-intensive endeavors (Fairley 2009, pp 6) where team members work co-operatively to achieve the project objective. Tom DeMarco calls this as "PeopleWare" given that staffing the "right" team members, and then managing them as a productive team is fraught with challenges such as specialization, attrition, autonomy, skill set obsolesce to name a few.

The level of intensity or the challenges in managing these five attributes varies depending on the type of project and the phase in the project [Remington and Oollack, 2008; Fairley, 2009]. The interaction of these five key elements in the project makes **deriving a reliable and validated software project measurement model a challenge.**

1.2.3 Lack of proven measures.

The history of software metrics is almost as old as the history of software engineering. The early efforts to implement software metrics for process improvements were often based on ad-hoc measurement programs which either concentrated on some key aspects of the products (such as defect counts) or came as a byproduct of other activities (such as counting Lines of count- LOC during compilation). According to Pfleeger et al, there is a discontinuity in measurement knowledge between software measurement researchers and practitioners. Software metrics researchers are usually more interested in validating theoretical concepts and conclusions, while practitioners usually want "few, quick and useful metrics" that have been empirically tested [Pfleeger, Ross, Curtis and Kitchenham, 1997].

Though there are a large number of measures that are researched, only a few have enjoyed any widespread use or acceptance in the real world. For example, according to Software Engineering Institute (SEI) there are 31 measures on product complexity [Mills, 1988]. But is there time available in the project to use all these 31 measures to measure complexity? Even worse, over 300 measures are identified for software development alone [Far, 2008]. According to Fenton, although there are a large number of measures available, only a few have enjoyed any widespread use of acceptance [Fenton, 2006]. **Hence most of the measurement models developed have little practical utility.**

1.3 The Research Problem and Questions

The three reasons mentioned in section 1.2 have ultimately resulted in the poor derivation and application of measurement programs in software projects where most decisions in software projects are done intuitively without understanding the complete picture of the project. Management visibility is a problem in software projects and this is one of the reasons for the poor success rate of software projects [Humphrey, 2005]. In this context, the research problem is **how to derive a generic, validated and objective measurement model reflecting the value propositions of stakeholders for improved decision making in software projects.**

The **relationship** in the above problem statement is between the measurement model and the value propositions of the stakeholders in software projects while the **population** is the stakeholders of software projects. The operational definition of **improved decision**

7

making reflects on the benefits of software metrics proposed by Watts Humphrey. According to him, software metrics in general can help in addressing the issues in software projects from four perspectives [Humphrey, 1999]:

1. **Understand:** Understand type metrics provide more insights about the software processes, products and services.
2. **Evaluate:** Evaluate type metrics are used in the decision-making process to study software products, processes or services in order to establish baselines and to determine if established standards, goals and acceptance criteria are being met.
3. **Control:** Control type metrics are used to monitor software processes, products and services and identify areas where corrective or management action is required.
4. **Predict:** Predict type metrics are used to estimate the values of base or derived measures in the future.

According to Ellis and Levy, for the research to be meaningful there has to be an identifiable connection between the answers to the research questions and the research problem [Ellis and Levy, 2008]. According to Maxwell, a good research question should direct the researcher to the information that will lead him or her to understand what he or she is set to investigate [Maxwell, 2005]. In this backdrop, considering that the research questions drive the type of study being conducted, the research problem gave rise to two research questions (RQ1 and RQ2).

- **RQ1:** How to scientifically derive a **generic and objective measurement model based on the varied and abstract value propositions of the software project stakeholders**?
- **RQ2:** What are the **validation criteria** the measurement model should be validated against? While scientifically deriving an effective measurement model is important, the measurement model should be validated so that measures in the model are well-grounded, relevant, meaningful, and logically correct.

Both RQ1 and RQ2 have both relational and casual attributes in them. In the relational study after describing the variables pertaining

8

to the measurement model, the objective is to identify the relationship between the variables. In a causal study the study helps us to determine whether one or more variables cause or affect the outcome variable in the measurement model.

1.4 Assumptions, Limitations and Delimitations in this research.

Any given research investigation will include assumptions, limitations and delimitation [Creswell, 2005]. According to Leedy and Ormrod, assumptions, limitations, and delimitations are critical components of a viable research [Leedy and Ormrod, 2005]. Assumption is basically a realistic expectation; something the researcher accepts as true without a concrete proof. Limitations are potential weaknesses or problems with the study identified by the researcher [Creswell, 2005, p. 198]. Delimitations refer to "what the researcher is not going to do" [Leedy and Ormrod, 2005]. While the assumptions and the limitations of this research are covered comprehensively in chapter 6 (in sections 6.2 and 6.3), this section covers the delimitations of this research. The purpose of listing out the delimitations at the outset is primarily to better manage the scope of the research. As the field of measurements in software engineering is vast, this research explicitly does not cover the following items.

- o New measures including the associated theory behind the measures will not be developed. There are many proven measures available that have been extensively researched. Hence no effort will be consciously made to identify new measures.

- o Though there is no universal agreement on how the software is categorized, it can be broadly classified into two types based on the field of application, namely: application software (which directly interacts with the users in such as word processing, accounting, purchasing et cetera.) and system software (which are programs used to start and run computer systems and networks including compilers and linkers which interface with the hardware). This research doesn't cover system software and looks at only application software commonly known as information systems (IS).

o Although software projects, programs and portfolios share some common characteristics, they are fundamentally different in terms of size, complexity, budget, resourcing et cetera. The proposed measurement model that will be developed and validated is exclusively for software projects.

o Subjective project measures are not in scope as they primarily depend on the viewpoint from which they are taken.

o The tools for capturing the data on the measures are not in scope. Most development editors have inbuilt tools and in addition there are numerous freeware tools available to compute product metrics. For the computation of project and process metrics, there are commercial software tools such as MS project, Primavera et cetera. Hence this research thesis does not attempt to come up with tools for managing the project data.

o Decision making rules from the measures. The objective of this research is to derive a measurement model to provide information for decision making for project stakeholders. The decision makers can use this measurement model to complement their experience and intuition and take appropriate corrective action based on the project situations.

1.5 Research Flow

According to Trochim, research is often conducted using the hourglass model structure. The hourglass model starts with a broad spectrum for research, focusing in on the required information through the methods (like the neck of the hourglass), then expands the research in the form of discussion and results [Trochim, 2006]. This research is organized on similar lines. This chapter is at the top end of the hourglass covering the elements of research such as background, problem, motivation and the goals of this research. Chapter 2 is the literature review based on the research questions to identify the critical issues and gaps in the current body of knowledge. Chapter 3 leverages the identified gaps in the literature review and formulates the research paradigm, design and methodology. It also covers the research method in the derivation of the generic and objective Goal-Question-Metric (GQM) based measurement model including the associated validation criteria that will be applied on the measurement model. Chapter 4 covers the analysis of the research – both the theoretical and empirical validation of the measurement model. This chapter also covers the data collection, sampling frame and samples for empirical validation and hypothesis testing. The research results i.e. the interpretation of the analysis including the contribution of this research are discussed in chapter 5. Finally, the assumptions, limitations and directions for future research are covered in chapter 6. The baseline questions used in GQM, the definition of the selected measures, the definitions of the validation criteria, the survey instrument and glossary are provided in the appendices. The entire "hour glass" research process including the traceability is as shown in the figure 1 below.

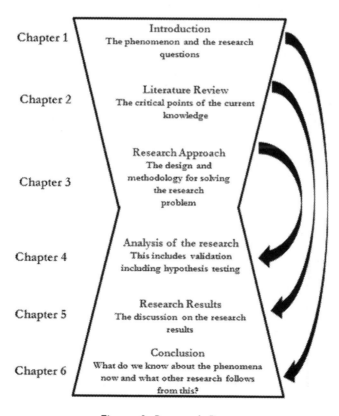

Figure 1: Research Process

1.6 Conclusion

Today speed of development, reduced cost and high quality are important elements for improved software project delivery. According to Peter Drucker, "What is measured improves" [Drucker, 2001]. In software project management, a reliable measurement can generate quantitative descriptions of products, processes and resources for formal modeling and evaluation at different phases of the SDLC. This helps to manage software projects better by knowing where the project currently stands so that suitable corrective actions can be taken for improvement. However the reliability of the software project measurement model can be improved if it reflects the varied and abstract value propositions of the stakeholders, encompasses the key characteristics of software project management, and is thoroughly validated – theoretically and empirically.

Chapter 2

Literature Review

2.1 Introduction

Invariably the research questions drive the literature review. The primary objective of literature review is to formulate the research approach based on what is currently known in the body of knowledge (BoK). In the context of this research, the primary impetus to address the two research questions (derived in chapter 1) is to enhance the chances of successfully delivering the software project with a measurement model so as to understand, evaluate, control and predict the outcome of the software project. Based on the two research questions the literature study critically reviews, synthesizes and analyzes the current BoK from peer reviewed papers, conference proceeding reports, journals, specialized books et cetera by accredited scholars and researchers.

2.2 Basics of Measurement Theory

Before getting into the core of the literature review, this section covers some basics aspects of measurement theory to understand some of the key terms that are used in this research thesis. Figure 2 below shows the software measurement process which is adapted from ISO/IEC 15939 where the key terms and concepts in this research are based upon.

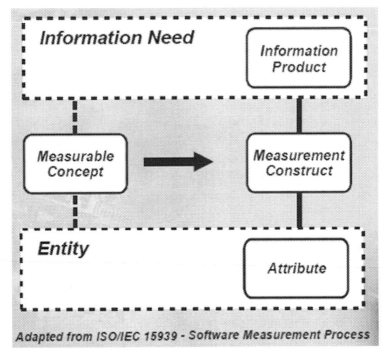

Figure 2: Software Measurement Process
[Figure adapted from ISO/IEC 15939]

Measurement refers to the art of assigning symbols or numbers to objects, events, people and characteristics according to a specific set of rules [Johnson and Christensen, 2004].Basically measurement theory is a branch of applied statistics that attempts to:

- Describe, categorize and evaluate the quality of measurements
- Improve the usefulness, accuracy and meaningfulness of measurements
- Propose methods for new and better measurement instruments
- Develop a good intuitive understanding of the concept that is being measured and modeling the intuitive understanding of the attribute in the measure.

Central to the software measurement process and measurement theory is the measurement construct. The measurement construct is a detailed structure that links the entity to be measured to a specified information need. The measurement construct describes how the relevant software attributes are quantified and converted to indicators to serve as a basis for decision making. A typical software measurement model has five levels as shown in the figure 3 below where the base measure, derived measure and indicator form the measurement construct.

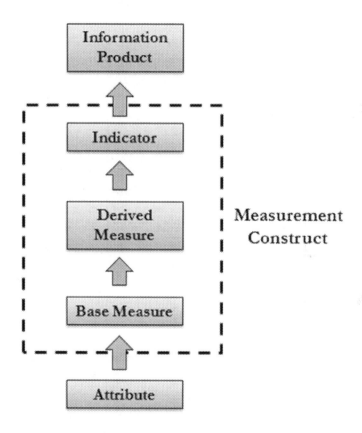

Figure 3: Measurement Model
[Figure adapted from ISO/IEC 15939]

Level 1: Attribute

The lowest level in the measurement model is the attribute. An attribute is a distinguishable property or characteristic of a software entity. An entity is basically the object that needs to be measured which in the context of this research is the software project. The entity can have sub-entities. For example in a software project, the sub-entities can include processes, products, and resources. There are two types of attributes an entity can possess.

1. Internal attribute: Attributes that the product itself exhibits, for example, the size of program [ISO/IEC,2007]
2. External attribute: Attributes those are dependent on the behavior of the system, for example, the reliability of a system is an external attribute [ISO/IEC, 2007].

Level 2: Base measure

A measure essentially maps an empirical attribute to the formal, mathematical world. A base measure is a measure of a single attribute defined by a specified measurement method. A base measure is functionally independent of all other measures and captures information about a single attribute. A base measure has five key characteristics [McGarry, John, Card, David, Jones, Cheryl, Beth Layman, Clark, Elizabeth, Dean, Joseph Dean, Hall, Fred, 2001].

1. Measurement Method

    This is a logical sequence of operations, used in quantifying an attribute with respect to a specified scale. The operations may involve activities such as counting occurrences or observing the event over passage of time.

2. Type of Method

    The type of measurement method depends on the nature of the operations used to quantify a particular attribute. There are two types of methods:

    *   Subjective—quantification involving human judgment or rating.

- Objective—quantification based on numerical rules.

3. Scale

   A scale is an ordered set of values, continuous or discrete, which the attribute is mapped. The scale defines the range of possible values that can be produced by executing the measurement method. The measurement method maps the magnitude of the measured attribute to a value on a scale.

4. Type of Scale

   A measurement scale is a quantitative metrical yardstick that provides measuring unit and scope for a specific type of attribute of objects [Wang, 2008]. The type of scale depends on the nature of the relationship between values on the scale. Four types of scales that are commonly defined are:

   - Nominal. It is categorical discrete data such as name of the program, type of project et cetera.
   - Ordinal. It is discrete rankings. Ordinal data have a natural ordering such as rank of defect unresolved days starting with the oldest defect. With ordinal data it is not possible to state with certainty whether the intervals between each value are equal.
   - Interval. It is numeric data. Interval data is like ordinal except that the intervals between each value are equally split. For example the difference between 300 and 600 LOC is same as the difference between 700 and 1000 LOC.
   - Ratio. It is also numeric data. It is essentially interval data with a natural zero point. For example, open defect count is ratio since zero defects is meaningful.

   The above four scale types namely - Nominal, Ordinal, Interval and Ratio have a distinct set of properties. At the nominal level have only categorization. At the ordinal level, one has the knowledge about the order of the categories along with categorization. With interval scales, the measure is not only classified and ordered but also defined how much the categories differ one from another. A ratio scale has all of these three characteristics as well as a non-arbitrary, or true, zero value. The amount of information present is as shown in the table 1 below and is the highest for the ratio scale measures.

Table 1: Information Level in Measurement Scales

Level of Measurement	Categorization	Order + Categorization	Set Intervals + Order + Categorization	True Zero + Set Intervals + Order + Categorization
Ratio	X	X	X	X
Interval	X	X	X	
Ordinal	X	X		
Nominal	X			

The key message from this table is each higher level of measurement scale provides additional information. In addition, most statistical techniques make sense when used with interval or ratio level measurement.

5. Unit of Measurement

    A unit of measurement is a particular quantity, with which other quantities of the same kind are compared in order to express their magnitude relative to that quantity. Only quantities expressed in the same units of measurement are directly comparable. Examples of units include the Giga-Hertz, Terabytes, et cetera.

Level 3: Derived Measure

A derived measure is a function of two or more base and/or derived measures. A derived measure captures information about more than one attribute. An example of a derived measure can be productivity which is derived by dividing the base measure of hours of effort by the base measure of lines of code (LOC). Closely associated with the derived measure is the measurement function which is an algorithm performed to combine two or more values of base and/or derived measures.

Level 4: Indicator

An indicator provides an evaluation of specified attributes derived from an analysis model with respect to defined information needs. Indicators are the basis for measurement analysis and decision making. Closely associated with the indicator are analysis model and decision criteria.

- Analysis model is an algorithm or calculation involving two or more base and/or derived measures with associated decision criteria. An analysis model is based on an understanding of the expected relationship between the measures and their behavior over time. The scale and method of measurement affect the choice of analysis techniques used to produce indicators. For example, it is not possible to compute the average of categorical or nominal data of a measure.
- Decision Criteria are numerical thresholds, variances, and control limits used to determine the need for action or further investigation or to describe the level of confidence in a given result. Decision criteria help to interpret the measurement results.

Level 5: Information Product

The Information Product is comprised of a collection of measurement constructs with interpretations

From the measurement construct perspective, the key components include measurement methods, base measures, measurement functions, derived measures, analysis models, decision criteria and indicators. Figure 4 depicts the relationship between these measurement construct components mathematically.

Indicator

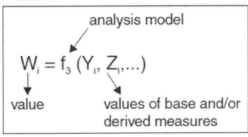

Derived Measure

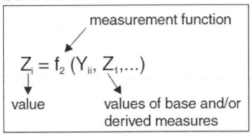

Base Measure

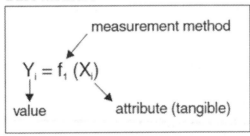

Figure 4: Mathematical description of Measurement Construct
[Figure adopted from McGarry et al, 2001]

2.3 Addressing the Research Questions

After reviewing the key measurement theory concepts, this section draws a link between the two research questions derived in chapter 1 and the current BoK. In chapter 1 two research questions that were identified were on two areas namely **generic and objective measurement**

model (RQ1) and **validation criteria** (RQ2). However the RQ1 has several dimensions such as:

○ Deriving a generic measurement model given the different types of software projects.

○ Project success criteria and time scales where the measurement model will be applied for software project performance. In other words when and what measures are needed to track the project for success or failure? For example, is the measurement model applicable till the scheduled project completion or later when the return-on-investment (ROI) and total cost of ownership (TCO) on the project are realized? Also closely related to the success criteria is the objective quantification of the "subjective" value propositions of the project stakeholders.

○ The selection of appropriate measurement framework to derive the measurement model for software projects given the plethora of frameworks available.

The literature review on RQ2 covers the validation criteria and the current measurement models. Essentially the literature review covers five areas pertaining to both RQ1 and RQ2. They are:

1. Definition of software project
2. Software project success criteria
3. Measurement frameworks
4. Metrics validation and
5. Current measurement models.

2.3.1 Definition of a Software Project

The discussion in this section is to identify the types of software projects for which the measurement model needs to be constructed. Software project management has evolved (and is still evolving) over years demonstrating different characteristics and demanding different management approaches for the delivery of software products. Today, the software projects that typically run inside an organization from an

Information system (IS) perspective can be classified into three types; regardless of the application being on Cloud or On-premise.

1. Commercial-off-the-Shelf (COTS) software projects

COTS software applications (also known as packaged applications) typically range from software development environments to operating systems, database management systems, and increasingly enterprise solutions. Typically, COTS systems have the following characteristics [Basili and Boehm, 2001]:

- The COTS applications come with a host of refined, feature rich, pre-configured and tested functionalities for most users of the application.
- These systems invariably offer rapid delivery of functionality to the end users, reduced development costs and fast application development and deployment.
- The buyer has limited access to source code.
- The vendor controls its product road map

COTS products are often considered as the "silver bullet" in software engineering offering significant savings in procurement, design, development, testing and maintenance. However the tradeoffs between COTS and be-spoke systems are development time v/s flexibility and control.

NOTE

With the advent of cloud computing, COTS systems can be an On-premise application or a Software-As-A-Service (SaaS) application.

2. Hybrid COTS software projects

The challenge in a typical "plug and play" COTS product is to understand what are the functionalities currently offered in COTS and to what extent they meet the project/intended requirements. COTS products are designed to meet the needs of a marketplace in general instead of satisfying the specific requirements of a particular organization. So in most cases these COTS applications need some "fine tuning" to adapt the functionality to the specific needs of the organization. For instance, in an accounts payable application, the standard COTS product might come up with say 100 functions while the requirement analyst has elicited 25 functions from the users. The challenge is to understand if these 25 functions are a subset of the 100 pre-configured functions and if so to what extent it meets the needs of the users. So hybrid COTS software projects fundamentally adapt the standard COTS product to the specific needs of the organization.

3. Bespoke software projects

The downside of relying on COTS is that the product is not tailored precisely to the business process and this can potentially affect in realizing the competitive advantage. In addition, non-development costs, such as licensing fees are significant and typically more than half the features in COTS software products go unused [Basili and Boehm, 2001]. Given the disadvantages in COTS products, bespoke software (commonly known as custom software) is a type of software that is developed for a particular organization for its specific needs. The two key advantages of be-spoke applications over COTS are [Dowling, 2000]:

- Control. In bespoke applications the customer can control the functionality, release schedule, upgrade path, et cetera.
- Visibility. Bespoke software can be examined to ensure it does not include any feature that jeopardizes security, safety, et cetera given than COTS is generally considered the "black box".

These two advantages make the bespoke application exclusive to the organization and can give the company a unique competitive advantage in the market at expense of significant more costs and implementation time.

The salient features of the three types of software projects are summarized as shown in the figure 5 below.

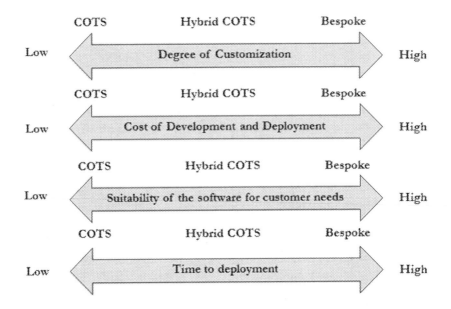

Figure 5: Comparison of the three types of software projects

In this backdrop, in a traditional software engineering approach, architectural decisions are based on business objectives, system requirements, assumptions, and constraints. But when it comes to COTS products, after system architecture plans are stabilized a set of COTS products are normally evaluated. According to Cecilia Albert and Lisa Brownsword of SEI (Software Engineering Institute) the requirements-driven software development lifecycle (SDLC) is not suitable for COTS products [Albert and Brownsword, 2002]. In addition the features provided by COTS influence the requirements and expectations of project and system stakeholders. For example, if a user wants to retrieve some information in a certain format, but COTS components only provide the information in a different format. Hence the key message is that conventional COTS products do not follow all phases of the SDLC process. In addition, according to Cechich and Piattini, the science of measuring COTS based systems (CBS) has not yet advanced to the point where there are standard measurement methods [Cechich and Piattini, 2004]. Hence the focus of this research will be to derive the measurement model for software projects which follows the complete SDLC (from inception to deployment). As COTS driven projects don't follow the complete SDLC, **the proposed measurement model will concentrate on hybrid COTS and bespoke software projects** giving an operational definition to the term "generic software project" in RQ1.

2.3.2 Software Project Success Criteria.

If a reliable measurement model can enhance the success of software project delivery, it is imperative to know the criteria under which the software projects will be considered successful. However despite Information Systems (IS) in general making a dramatic impact on the business operation, organizations are hard pressed to evaluate the success of their IS investments [Delone and Mclean, 2003]. The common assessment of success on IS or software projects is that it is delivered on time, to budget and it meets the specification of the project stakeholders. For instance the CHAOS report from Standish is based on the feedback from senior management primarily on schedule and budget on the software project success [Standish, 2009]. However, this is taking a narrow view of how a project is measured. The IS project success should extend beyond technological performance, cost and duration to dimensions such as user/stakeholder satisfaction and benefits [Thomas and Fernandez, 2008]. The criteria for IS or software project success should be much wider, incorporating the views of all stakeholders in the software project [Wateridge, 1998].

However the criteria for software project success or more specifically the derivation of measures from the stakeholders' perspectives is extremely complex as the value propositions of the stakeholders are generally abstract, implicit and combines different levels of expectations over different timescales for different types of results as shown in table 2 below [Turner et al, 2009].

Table 2: Expectations of the Project Stakeholders

Results	Project Output	Project Outcome	Impact
Time Scale	**End of Project**	**Plus Months**	**Plus Years**
Stakeholder			
Users	Features	Usability	New technology
	Performance	Convenience	New capability
	Documentation	Reliability and Availability	New competence
	Training	Maintainability	New class
			Job security
Project sponsor and management	Features	Performance	Future projects
	Performance	Benefits and Reputation	New technology
	Time and cost	Relationships	New capability
	Completed work	Investor Loyalty	New competence and class
Project Manager and Project team	Time and cost	Reputation	Job security
	Performance	Relationship	Future projects
	Learning	Repeat business	New Technology
	Camaraderie		New competence
	Retention		
	Well being		
Suppliers	Time and cost	Performance	Future business
	Performance	Reputation	New technology
	Profit	Relationship	New competence
	Client appreciation	Repeat business	Whole life social cost-benefit ratio
	Safety record, Environmental impact	Environmental impact	
	Completed work	Social costs and benefits	

Given the exhaustive list of above measures, when are these measures relevant in a software project? For instance the "Repeat business" measure might be more relevant when the project is completed and Return on Investment (ROI) and Total Cost of Ownership (TCO) are realized while "time and cost" are definitely the measures for project tracking during the project execution. This brings us to the next discussion - **when do the stakeholders consider the project a success or a failure so that appropriate project measures can be derived to make the conclusion?** When is that critical time period? Is it immediately after the scheduled completion date or later when the ROI or TCO on the project is realized? According to Darren Dalcher project outcomes should be a function of time scales, organization levels and goals (of the stakeholders) and a project can be seen as successful at four levels as shown in the table 3 below [Dalcher, 2009].

Table 3: Dalcher's definition of software project success

Level	Type	Critical Success Factors
1	Project Management Success	Efficiency and Performance
2	Project Success	Objectives, Benefits, Stakeholders
3	Business Success	Value Creation and Delivery
4	Future Potential	New Market, Skills, Opportunities

While levels 1 and 2 emphasize the delivery of the project, levels 3 and 4 encourage long term strategic thinking i.e. they look beyond individual projects where measures such as "repeat business" and "relationship" are relevant. Level 1 looks at the project management processes while level 2 covers the software development lifecycle (SDLC) and project management lifecycle (PMLC) catering to the stakeholder's objectives and benefits. Hence the focus of this research will be at level 1 and 2. In addition, technological and business changes are so rampant in software industry that measuring a software project say two years from the project completion date for business success (level 3) and future potential (level 4) is farfetched. A classic example would be a standard feature turning into a defect a few years later because of changing business conditions or industry standards or even new government regulations. So elements of the software project success should encompass the process elements as well.

This brings to the final element — what are the criteria for the IS/ software project success (or failure)? According to Delone and Mclean, success in software projects involves six dimensions — system quality, information quality, service quality, intention to use, user satisfaction, and net benefits [Delone and Mclean, 2003]. The six dimensions in the model known as the D&M IS Success model are:

- System quality measures the desired characteristics such as functionality, availability, reliability, adaptability, response time et cetera.
- Information quality ensures that the application is personalized, complete, relevant, easy to understand, and secure
- Service quality is the overall support delivered in running the application.
- Usage measures everything from navigation, to information retrieval, to execution of a transaction.
- User satisfaction covers the entire customer experience
- Net benefits captures the balance of positive and negative impacts of the application on the entire eco-system including the customers, suppliers, employees, organizations, markets to name a few

These six dimensions are interrelated with important implications for the measurement, analysis and reporting [Delone and Mclean, 2003]. The D&M IS success model is as shown in figure 6 below.

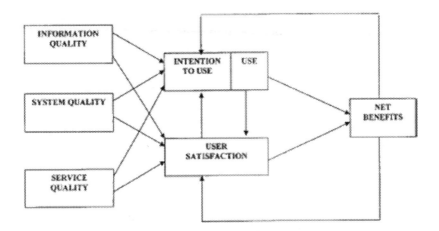

Figure 6: D&M IS Success Model
[Figure adapted from Delone and Mclean, 2003]

Synthesizing the research done by the above mentioned researchers **the software project measurement model should encompass the needs and expectations of all the stakeholders** during the **duration of the project** satisfying the **six dimensions of the D&M IS success model.** This relationship is as shown in figure 7 below.

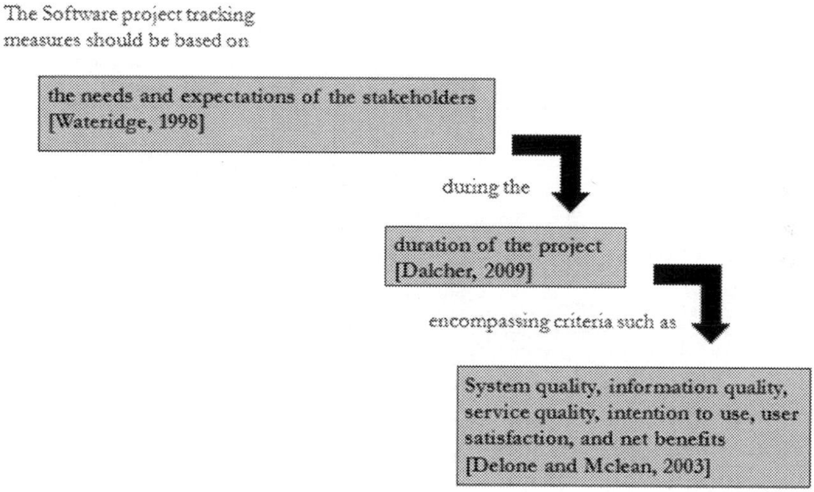

The Software project tracking measures should be based on

the needs and expectations of the stakeholders [Wateridge, 1998]

during the

duration of the project [Dalcher, 2009]

encompassing criteria such as

System quality, information quality, service quality, intention to use, user satisfaction, and net benefits [Delone and Mclean, 2003]

Figure 7: Software Project Success Criteria

2.3.3. Overview of Measurement frameworks.

Several measurement frameworks have emerged in recent years including some organizational frameworks that have an integrated measurement methodology embedded within them. Figure 8 below illustrates the chronology of measurement frameworks relevant to software projects.

Dr. Prashanth Harish Southekal

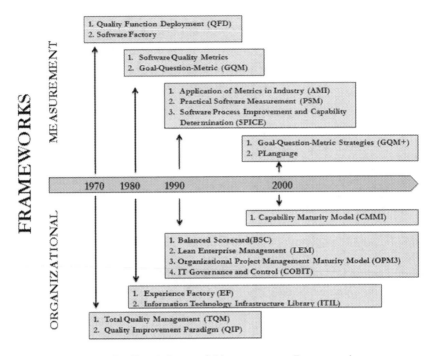

Figure 8: Chronology of Measurement Frameworks

Even though several approaches to software measurement have been proposed such as goal–oriented approaches, axiomatic approaches, structure based approaches, algebraic approaches, rule based approaches et cetera, the goal–oriented approaches for software measurement are commonly used because they use stakeholder goals, objectives and strategies with appropriate mechanisms to analyze data in a systematic way. Stakeholder goals are very important in the formulation of the measurement model as project management including software project management is strongly stakeholder driven [Smith, 2000].

According to Basili, Lindvall, Regardie, Seaman, Heidrich, Munch, Rombach and Trendowicz most of the approaches attempting to align measurement with the business and software are combinations of three well-known approaches to measurement i.e., Balanced Scorecard (BSC), Goal-Question-Metric (GQM), and Practical Software Measurement (PSM) [Basili, Lindvall, Regardie, Seaman, Heidrich, Munch, Rombach and Trendowicz, 2007]. BSC focuses on the business vision from four concrete perspectives- Financial, Customer, Internal business processes and Learning and growth and PSM provide a set of 75 pre-defined measures. GQM defines the strategic goals reflecting stakeholder needs. The following sections critically examines each of the three goal oriented measurement frameworks (GMFs).

1. Balanced Scorecard (BSC)

The Balanced scorecard (BSC) provides measures for project or organizational performance across four perspectives: Financial, Customer, Internal business processes and Learning and growth [Kaplan and Norton, 1992]. The term "scorecard" signifies quantified performance measures and "balanced" signifies that the system is balanced between:

- Short and long term objectives
- Financial and Non-financial measures
- Lagging and leading indicators
- Internal and external performance perspectives.

The key characteristic of the BSC is the presentation of holistic measures where each measure is compared against a 'target' value within a single concise report. BSC does not provide a static set of measures, but serves as a framework for choosing measures, processes, and initiatives that are aligned with organizational vision, strategy and business goals. The idea is to create specific and actionable linkages among the four perspectives so that all project activities contribute to a unified vision and strategy to help projects/organizations align business activities, improve internal and external communications, and monitor organization performance [Kaplan and Norton, 1992]. In a well-designed scorecard, the four perspectives form a chain of cause-effect relationships. For example learning and growth leads to better business/project processes resulting in higher user/customer satisfaction and thus a higher return on investment (ROI).The figure 9 below shows how the four perspectives and the four parameters fit together and interact.

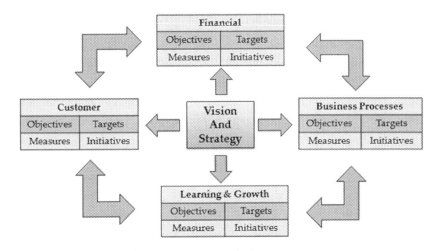

Figure 9: Balanced Scorecard
[Figure adopted from Kaplan and Norton, 1992]

Within each of the four perspectives, BSC emphasis the following four parameters:

- **Objectives**: It is the goal to be achieved in that particular perspective
- **Measures**: How the progress for that particular objective will be measured
- **Targets**: The target is the goal sought for each measure
- **Initiatives**: The actions that will be taken to reach the target.

The key strengths of BSC are:

1. Strong top management focus.
2. Links various company aspects under one management system. It aligns individual goals to the objectives of the organization/project.
3. Links measurement to the organization's vision and goals.

The disadvantages of BSC are:

1. BSC is focused on the needs of upper management.

2. The four areas in BSC are abstract and do not mention any specific measures. It gives very little support for project level measurement definition.

3. BSC is generic and not specific to software projects.

2. Practical Software Measurement (PSM)

PSM is information driven measurement process which offers detailed guidance on software measurement to link issues, measurement categories, and measures [Florac, William, Park, Robert and Carleton, Anita, 1997]. It is essentially a issue-based measurement method, guiding software project managers to select, collect, define, analyze and report scientific software issues such as risks, defects et cetera. The three concepts that form the foundation of PSM are [Card and Jones, 2003]:

1. **Information needs of Project Managers.**

   The information needs drive the selection of the measures to influence the outcome of the project. The information needs in turn is derived from the goals the project manager seeks to achieve and the obstacles that hinder the achievement of the goals.

2. **The Measurement Information Model (MIM).**

   Once the goals and obstacles are identified, the next step is to define the MIM. The MIM provides a formal relationship between the information needs and the objective data to be collected; commonly called measures.

3. **The Measurement Process Model.**

   An effective measurement process must address the selection of appropriate measures with an effective analysis of the corresponding data that is collected. The measurement process model tackles this through four iterative measurement activities: establish, plan, perform, and evaluate as shown in figure 10 below [Card and Jones, 2003].

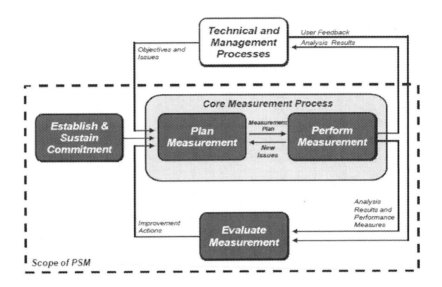

Figure 10: PSM Measurement Process Model
[Figure adopted from Card and Jones, 2003]

The key benefits of PSM are:

1. Project initiates the measurement activities.
2. Project characteristics guide the measure/metric selection.
3. Assesses measurement activities as part of the framework.

The short comings of PSM are:

1. PSM does not create a direct link between the measures and business goals. It sees measurement as project level activity only.
2. PSM is primarily a measurement tool for project managers and not a measurement framework for all stakeholders in the project.
3. PSM focuses on using existing 75 measures/indicators repositories based on various information categories to know the project status. The challenges here are:
    • Implementing this complete metrics suite will consume a lot of time in data collection, analysis and implementation.

- Even if a small set of measures is carved out, it is still not appropriate for other stakeholders as the 75 measures are essentially designed for the project managers.
4. PSM was developed specifically by US Department of Defense (DoD) based on experiences of software projects run by the Defense department. It is not generic as it is not a measurement framework coming out from the software industry practitioners.

3. Goal-Question-Metric (GQM)

Goal-Question-Metric (GQM) method was formulated by Victor Basili, Caldiera Gianluigi and Deiter Rombach in 1994 [Basili, Gianluigi and Rombach, 1994]. The GQM approach provides a method for defining goals, refining them into questions and formulating metrics for data collection, analysis and decision making. It focuses on getting the right people involved at all levels to ensure the right goals and metrics are identified. Fundamentally GQM is based on eight principles namely:

1. **Goal-driven:** Define measurement goals in line with the project goals.
2. **Context-sensitive:** Consider context/environment when defining measurement goals.
3. **Top-down:** Refine goals top-down into measures via questions.
4. **Documented:** Document measurement goals and their refinement explicitly.
5. **Bottom-up:** Analyze and interpret the collected data bottom-up in the context of the goal.
6. **People-oriented:** Actively involve all stakeholders in the measurement program.
7. **Sustained:** Measure for systematic and continuous software process improvement (SPI).
8. **Reuse-oriented:** Describe the context to facilitate packaging and reuse of knowledge gained.

The result of the application of the GQM approach is a measurement system targeting a particular set of issues and a set of rules for the interpretation of the measurement data. The resulting measurement model has three levels:

1. **Conceptual level (Goal)**

A goal describes the purpose of the measurement and is defined for an object with respect to various models of quality, from various points of view and relative to a particular environment.

2. **Operational level (Question)**

A set of questions is used to characterize the achievement of a specific goal. The questions generated should define the goals in a quantifiable way. The questions are at the operational level and help to clarify and refine the goal and to capture the variation of understanding of the goals that exists among the different stakeholders.

3. **Quantitative level (Metric)**

A set of metrics/measures is associated with every question in order to answer it in a measurable or quantitative way. The measures specified should be collected to answer the questions and track process and product conformance to the goals.

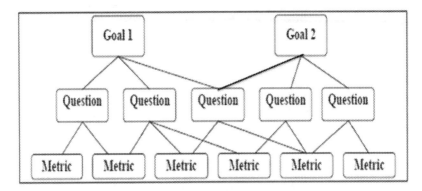

Figure 11: GQM Model
[Figure adopted from Basili et al, 1994]

As illustrated in the figure 11 [Basili et al, 1994], the mapping among goals, questions and metrics is not one-to-one. For each goal, there can be several questions and the same question can be linked to multiple goals as deemed appropriate. For each question, there can be multiple metrics, and some metrics may be applicable to more than one question. Adherence to and preservation of this hierarchical structure helps ensure that the measurement program focuses on the right metrics and that we avoid extra work associated with collecting metrics that are not really needed.

The strengths of GQM are:

1. Builds a visible link between measurement goals and measures.
2. Creates a detailed measurement plan including the data to be collected.
3. Involves all stakeholders in measurement definition, implementation and analysis.

The weaknesses of GQM are:

1. GQM doesn't provide explicit support for integrating its software measurement model with the larger element of the organization such as business goals, strategies and assumptions.
2. Creates too much flexibility and not enough guidance. For instances in formulating the questions, GQM does not provide guidance on when to terminate.
3. GQM does not bring uniqueness. For the same goal(s) and questions of the stakeholders there could be more than one set of measures.

As explained above, each of the three goal-oriented measurement frameworks (GMF) i.e. BSC, PSM and GQM have their own pros-and-cons. Table 4 below summarizes the key advantages and disadvantages of the three GMFs.

Table 4: Comparison of the three GMFs.

GMF	Advantage	Disadvantage
BSC	Links various company aspects under one management system. It aligns each goal to the objectives of the organization.	It is abstract, focused on upper management needs and gives very little support for project level measurement definition.
PSM	Project characteristics guide the measure selection from the pool of 75 measures.	As it focuses on using existing 75 measures to know the project status, the challenges are: • Implementing this complete metrics suite will consume a lot of time in data collection and analysis. • Even if a small set of measures is carved out, it will still be not relevant for other project stakeholders as the 75 measures are essentially designed for the project managers.
GQM	Involves all organization stakeholders in measurement definition, implementation and analysis.	Creates too much flexibility and not enough guidance. For instances in formulating the questions, it does not provide guidance on when to terminate. In addition, GQM does not bring uniqueness. For the same goal(s) and questions of the stakeholders there could be more than one set of measures.

After evaluating the above three goal oriented measurement frameworks, the challenge is which measurement framework to adopt for deriving the measurement model for software projects.

2.3.4 Validation of Measurement Models.

Irrespective of the measurement framework adopted, the measurement model derived should be validated against a set of criteria. Fundamentally validation is not a binary trait, but rather a degree of confidence. The ISO/IEC definition of validation is "confirmation, through the provision of objective evidence, that the requirements for a specific intended use or application have been fulfilled" [ISO/IEC, 2007]. Validity ensures that the test is measuring what is intended to be measured in the given context and that the interpretations made on the basis on the scores are correct. Validation is therefore an enquiry process of gathering validity evidence for the soundness and relevance of the inferences. Though there are different types of validity evidence, the best rule is to collect multiple sources of evidence as more validity evidence one has, more is the confidence in the results placed. In the recent years, however, the thinking on the validity issues has moved from the discussions on the types of validity (i.e. content, criterion, and construct validity) to methods on obtaining evidence for unitary evidence. Essentially in contemporary usage, all validity is construct validity, which requires multiple sources of evidence [Downing, 2003].

Metric validation is ensuring that a metric is acceptable by the community in both interpretation and use because it is well-grounded, relevant, meaningful, and logically correct [Meeneley, Smith and Williams 2010]. From the software measurement perspective, for a strong validation the measurement model must be validated theoretically and empirically [Braind, EL Emam and Morasca, 1996]. Theoretical validation tells us if a measure is valid with respect to certain defined criteria from measurement theory, while empirical validation provides evidences from real world instances. Neither kind of validation is sufficient by itself and both theoretical and empirical validation must be carried out to avoid the problem of defining a theoretically sound measure which is otherwise useless in its practical application [Braind et al, 1995].

However, before the measures are validated, the measures should be clearly defined. For example, according to Briand, concepts such as complexity and size are very often subject to interpretation and appear to have inconsistent definitions in the literature [Briand, 1994]. As a consequence, there is a need to unambiguously define the measures which can be used to track software projects. One way of doing so is to define precisely the mathematical properties of the measures using measurement theory and theoretical validation determines if the measures follow concepts from measurement theory. Figure 12 below shows the structural model of measurement showing the relationship between empirical and mathematical elements.

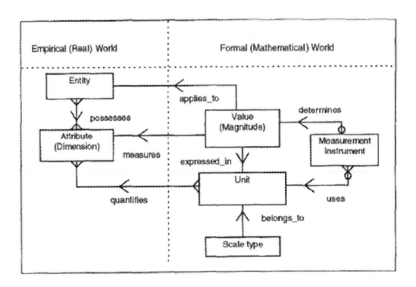

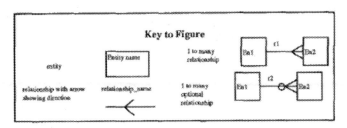

Figure 12: Structural Model of Measurement
[Figure adopted from Kitchenham et al, 1995]

However, what constitutes the software metrics validation criteria has been intensely debated for almost half a century and researchers have not yet reached a consensus on this system of rules because no researcher has provided a "proper discussion of relationships among different approaches to metrics validation" [Kitchenham et al, 1995]. Instead, software metric researchers have often been proposing their own, specialized means of validation. For instance the top 20 cited papers in the field of "software metrics" in the last 2 decades from Google scholar, IEEE Xplore and ACM Digital library involved significant cross-referencing, discussion, and disagreement as shown in the figure 13 below [Meneely et al, 2010].

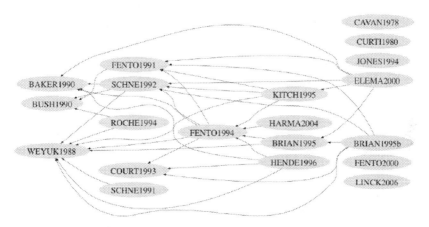

Figure 13: Citation Network
[Figure adopted from Meneely et al, 2010]

Hence, in the absence of a generalized and accepted validation approach it is essential to **find the theoretical and empirical validation criteria the measurement model should be validated against to address the research question RQ2 on validation criteria.**

2.3.5 Current Measurement Models

According to Norman Fenton, software metrics research has failed almost totally in terms of industrial penetration [Fenton, 2006]. There are numerous measurement models that are currently available. Specifically we have COCOMO and SLIM (for effort estimation), Function point models (for size), reliability growth models, complexity models et cetera. In addition to the D&IM IS success model discussed earlier, many researchers have proposed generic and detailed software measurement models. Examples include:

- Everald Mills from SEI proposes that a software project measurement model should include at least the four base measures i.e. size, schedule, cost and quality [Mills, 1988].
- Steve McConnell identifies size, productivity (schedule and cost), defects, maintainability and quality as useful metrics in a software project [McConnell, 1993]. He further proposes some measures such as number of blank lines, severity of each defect, Lines of code (LOC) in each routine et cetera which he states have helped practitioners in software projects.
- According to Moller and Paulish, the five widely used measurements are size, defects, change requests, deviation from schedule and deviation from productivity [Moller and Paulish, 1993].
- According to Larry Putnam, the measures underlying effective software management are effort, time, size, and quality. [Putnam and Meyers, 2002].
- Stephen H. Kan classifies software metrics into three categories: product metrics, process metrics, and project metrics. Product metrics describe the characteristics of the product such as size, complexity, design features, performance, and quality level. Process metrics describe the software development lifecycle process. Examples include the effectiveness of defect removal during development, the pattern of testing defect arrival, and the response time of the fix process. Project metrics give more details on the project usually on schedule, cost and quality. Examples include the staffing pattern in the project, cost, schedule, and productivity [Kan, 2003].
- Bill Curtis and Capers Jones have defined five major desirable characteristics in the software product to provide business value [Curtis and Jones, 2009]. The five measures are:
  1. Reliability: Reliability measures the level of risk and the likelihood of potential application failures including the defects injected due to modifications made to the software.
  2. Efficiency: The source code and software architecture attributes are the elements that ensure high performance once the application is in run-time mode. Efficiency is especially important for applications where performance and scalability are paramount. An analysis of source code efficiency and

scalability provides a clear picture of the latent business risks and the harm they can cause to the business.

3. Security: A measure of the likelihood of potential security breaches due to poor coding and architectural practices. This quantifies the risk of encountering critical vulnerabilities that damage the business.

4. Maintainability: Maintainability includes the notion of adaptability, portability and transferability (from one development team to another). Measuring and monitoring maintainability is a must for mission-critical applications where change is driven by tight time-to-market schedules and where it is important for IT to remain responsive to business-driven changes. It is also essential to keep maintenance costs under control.

5. Size: While not a quality attribute per se, combined with the above quality characteristics, software size can be used to assess the amount of work produced and to be done by teams, as well as their productivity through correlation with time-sheet data, and other SDLC-related metrics.

Below table 5 gives the analysis of the above measurement models.

Table 5: Comparison of Measurement Models

Measure/ Attribute	Mills	McConnell	Putnam	Moller and Paulish	Kan	Curtis and Jones
Size	X	X	X	X	X	X
Complexity or Maintainability		X			X	X
Schedule	X	X	X	X	X	
Cost	X	X	X	X	X	
Quality	X	X	X		X	X

However these measurement models have three major issues.

- **None of the above measurement models are explicitly derived from stakeholder analysis.**

Software Project management is heavily stakeholder dependent and stakeholder analysis helps identifying the individuals or groups that are likely to affect or be affected by the project. A stakeholder analysis based measurement model will weigh and balance the competing demands of the stakeholders in addressing the project goals.

- **No focus on measure.**

For instance when Larry Putnam and Steve McConnell talk about size, it is abstract and subjective and not a measure such as Lines of Code (LOC) or Function Points (FP) which are concrete and objective. Similarly when SEI or Mills talks about quality, it is not very specific. Applying these measures gives rise to fundamental questions such as definition of quality, size et cetera. Also when Moller and Paulish talk about productivity it is raises further questions such as – is it the developer productivity (say defects/KLOC) or the investment from the software application itself as return on investment (ROI) and total cost of ownership (TCO). On a similar vein, the problem with the measurement model of Curtis and Jones is also abstractness in the five measures. For instance does reliability measure the complexity of algorithms or does it measure the data integrity in the applications? Does efficiency measure memory/disk space management or coding practices for SQL queries on indexing on large tables while looping? Basically using "abstract" measures such as quality, size, maintainability et cetera will encourage stakeholders to interpret them in their own context with meanings that may differ from the intended or standard definition.

- **Lack of a standardized mapping system.**

The selection, definition, and consistent use of a mapping system for the selected measure are critical to a successful metrics program. However even for simple measures such as LOC, no standard counting method has been widely accepted.

Do developers count physical or logical lines of code? Do developers count comments or data definition statements? Another example is quality in a project – how is quality defined, tracked and improved?

In this backdrop, the measurement model should be based on stakeholder value propositions where each measure in the measurement model is clearly defined for consistent interpretation.

2.4 Conclusion

Reflecting on section 2.3, the literature review provided the following road map.

SI #	Literature Review themes	Outcomes
1	Software project definition	The research shall focus on deriving a measurement model for hybrid COTS and bespoke software projects
2	Software project success criteria measures	The measurement model shall encompass the needs and expectations of all stakeholders during the duration of the software project satisfying the six dimensions of D&M IS success model
3	Measurement frameworks	The literature studies came up with three measurement frameworks to consider. The subsequent chapters will explore more.
4	Metrics Validation	The literature studies did not come up with defined validated criteria for theoretical and empirical validation. Though Meenley et al identified 47 measures it was not specific to software projects and included extensive cross referencing and disagreement.
5	Current measurement models	The six measurement models are not based on stakeholder value propositions, are abstract and lack a standardized mapping system.

Of the five research themes identified for literature review, themes 1, 2 and 5 gave a clear direction. However themes 3 and 4, which form the crux of this research thesis, provided a roadmap for carry out further investigation which is covered in the next chapter. Essentially literature review pertains to two dimensions; information seeking to account for what has been published and critical appraisal to identify unbiased and valid studies. The literature review points to some fundamental issues and gaps in the current body of knowledge (BoK) in the field of software project measurement. While numerous measurement frameworks and models are available, there is no one framework and model that is recommended/validated during the project duration for hybrid COTS and bespoke type software projects considering the stakeholder value propositions. While some researchers have proposed measurement models, these models are not based on stakeholder analysis and lack clear definition and details for effective implementation in the software project. The next chapter leverages the research questions and gaps identified till now to build the research paradigm, design and the methodology for the research thesis.

Chapter 3

Research Approach – The Paradigm, Design and Methodology

3.1 Introduction

Software project management is a multi-disciplinary field crossing social and technological boundaries. Hence it is imperative to understand not only how software products are built, but also to know how teams and organizations coordinate the efforts. Hence research strategies should be drawn from disciplines that study both systems and human behaviors both at individual (for example psychology) and at the team and organizational levels (for example sociology).

This chapter covers the research approach undertaken based on the two research questions and the gaps identified in the literature review. The research approach encompasses research paradigm, design and methodology. This chapter starts with the research paradigm, explores into the design elements and then in the research methodology section, the measurement framework for a software project is selected. From the measurement framework the measurement model including the measures is derived. From the measures in the measurement model, the software project metrics validation criteria are then formulated for both theoretical and empirical validation.

3.2 Research Paradigm

The research paradigm in this thesis is basically characterized through their ontology (what is reality?), epistemology (what can be known?) and methodology (How to go about finding out?) mixing the positivist (objective) and interpretative (subjective) perspectives. These three building blocks of research i.e. ontology, epistemology and methodology interact with each other as shown in the figure 14 below creating a holistic view of how the knowledge pertaining to software project metrics is viewed, applied and discovered [Guba, 1990].

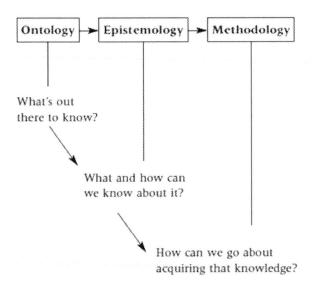

Figure 14: Building Blocks of Research
[Figure adapted from Hay, 2002, p. 64]

Given that Information systems (IS) are composed of people, structures, technologies, and work systems, figure 15 below presents the conceptual framework with three major components i.e. environmental, research and knowledge base for understanding, executing, and evaluating IS research [Henver, 2004]. The first component in the figure, i.e. environment is composed of people, organizations, and their existing or planned technologies define the problem space. The second component i.e. IS research comprises two basic approaches:

behavioral science research (BSR) focusing primarily on developing and justifying theories and design science research (DSR) to create IT artifacts intended to solve organizational problems. The goal of BSR is truth and the goal of DSR is utility. The third component i.e. knowledge base is composed of foundations and methodologies providing the raw materials through which IS research is accomplished.

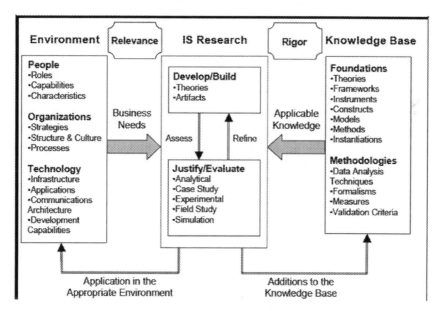

Figure 15: IS Research Framework
[Figure adapted from Henver et al, 2004]

Applying the IS research framework of Henver with the three generic building blocks of research, the research paradigm for this thesis is as shown in the table 6 below pertaining to the research questions on measurement model (RQ1) and validation criteria (RQ2). The research perspectives are characterized by two dominant philosophical stances – positivism and interpretivism. Positivism states that knowledge must be based on logical inference from a set of verifiable observable facts and is guided primarily by scientific or objective criteria such as quantification, systematic collection of evidence, reliability and transparency. Interpretivists argue that logic methods of natural sciences should be separated from human context so as to understand the subjective experiences of those being studied, how they think and feel, and how they act in their natural contexts.

Table 6: Research Paradigm elements

Research Elements	Research Areas (Research Question)	Research Perspective	
		Positivist/Objective	Interpretative/Subjective
Ontology (What is reality?)	Measurement Model (RQ1)	The measurement model will be based on the measurement framework. Though there are numerous measurement frameworks, the GQM, PSM and BSC measurement frameworks are goal driven and found to be suitable for software projects [Basili et al, 2007].	Derivation of the measurement model should encompass: • Value propositions of the project stakeholder during the duration of the project • Totality of the situation such as type of software project and the criteria for project success.
	Validation Criteria (RQ2)	Even today there is still no consensus on what constitutes the software project metrics validation criteria. For instance, the top 20 cited software metrics papers involve significant cross-referencing, discussion, and disagreement [Meenley et al, 2010].	
Epistemology (What can be known?)	Measurement Model (RQ1)	Derivation of the objective measures for tracking during the entire SDLC for hybrid and bespoke software projects.	Selection of the appropriate measurement framework for software projects and the current measurement models.
	Validation Criteria (RQ2)	Validation criteria on measures involving both theoretical and empirical criteria.	

Methodology (How to go about finding out?)	Measurement Model (RQ1)		Derivation of the measurement model should involve a mix of stakeholder participation, hermeneutical (interpretation) and dialectical (argument) approaches.
	Validation Criteria (RQ2)	The analysis of the criteria can be quantitative or statistical approaches.	Derivation and analysis of the validation criteria should include a mix of hermeneutical and dialectical approaches.

3.3 Research Design

Research design ensures that the evidence obtained from the research enables one to answer the research questions as unambiguously as possible. Leveraging the research paradigm which was explained in section 3.2, the research design in this thesis is consists of major four steps. Step 1 is identifying the right measurement framework for software projects based on positivist and interpretative perspectives. In step 2, the measurement framework selected is applied to derive the measurement model concerning the value propositions of the stakeholders at different time scales for software project success. This step was primarily subjective encompassing a mix of stakeholder participation, hermeneutical and dialectical perspectives. Once the measurement model was formulated, step 3 derives the validation criteria - both theoretical and empirical. The primary objective of theoretical validation is to minimize the chances of failure encountered during the implementation of the measurement model by addressing exceptions. After the validation criteria were derived, in step 4 ten questions of Cem Kaner and Walter Bond were applied for compliance on the measurement model to bolster theoretical validation providing a hermeneutical perspective [Kaner and Bond, 2004]. Empirical validation which forms the crux of the validation exercise was carried out with mixed research which includes the application of quantitative and qualitative methods mixing the positivist (with survey) and interpretative (with case study) perspectives. The rationale of going for mixed research with quantitative and qualitative methods for empirical validation was for two main reasons.

    ○   As mentioned in the research paradigm section acquiring knowledge in an IS or software project management context requires the application of behavioral science research (BSR) through quantitative methods and design science research (DSR) using qualitative methods [Hevner, March, Park, and Sudha, 2004]. This philosophy is further empirically validated by the fact that between 1991 and 2001, 77% of IS research methods included surveys (41%) and case studies (36%) [Chen and Hirschheim, 2004].

    ○   Bolster the principle of triangulation where validation is not reliant on a single research method. According to Johnson and Christensen, researchers should mix methods to provide complementary strengths and non-overlapping weaknesses [Johnson and Christensen, 2004]. McGrath notes that there is no single research method that achieves all the three research objectives of generalizability, precision in control and measurement and existential realism. He proposes that the only way to mitigate the apparent weaknesses of any one methodology is through application of several methodologies to the research problem [McGrath 1982]. Basically mixing quantitative and qualitative methods complement each other as shown in the table 7 below [Gable, 1994].

Table 7: Strengths and Weakness of Qualitative and Quantitative Methods

Parameter	Qualitative Method Ex: Case Study	Quantitative Method Ex: Survey
Controllability	Low	Medium
Deductability	Low	Medium
Repeatability	Low	Medium
Generalizability	Low	High
Discoverability	High	Medium
Representability	High	Medium

The high level research design/methodology that will be applied in this thesis is as shown in figure 16 below.

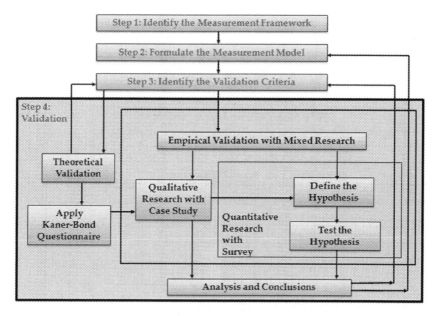

Figure 16: Research Design

3.4 Research Methodology

Software metrics researchers and practitioners have proposed that a robust software measurement model should encompass both formulation and validation – theoretical and empirical [Braind, 1995; Fenton, 2006; Soni, Shrivastava and Kumar, 2009]. As mentioned in the research paradigm section, the formulation of the measurement model focuses on understanding the problem (Behavioral science research) while the validation focuses on solving the problem (Design science research). Based on this, the research methodology is split into four steps in line with the research design explained in section 3.3.

3.4.1: Step 1- Identification of the Measurement Framework

The first step was to identify the measurement framework so that the measurement model can be derived. Of the three goal-oriented measurement frameworks (GMF) i.e. BSC, PSM and GQM, GQM was found to be the most appropriate measurement framework for software projects as shown below in table 8 [Sirvio, 2003].

Table 8: Comparison of goal-oriented measurement frameworks (GMF)

SI #	Critical Success Factor Questions	GQM	PSM	BSC
1	Does the method support participation of all affected parties?	X	X	X
2	Does the method support co-operation with software engineers?	X	X	
3	Does the method support planning and carrying out training as part of the initiative?		X	
4	Does the method support commitment of top managers?			X
5	Does the method support commitment of middle managers?			X
6	Does the method support commitment of software engineers?			
7	Does the method support that improved solutions are developed on a case-by-case basis?	X	X	X
8	Does the method support that the current status of processes is clarified?	X		
9	Does the method support that the link between business and improvement goals is established?			X
10	Does the method ensure measurement goals are based on needs and well understood?	X		X
11	Does the method ensure that detailed measurement plan is generated?	X	X	X

12	Does the method support developed solutions are tested in a pilot project?	X	X	
13	Does the method ensure that practical support is always available for development projects?	X		
14	Does the method support using metrics in monitoring improvement actions and results?	X	X	X
15	Does the method support sustainability of an improvement initiative?	X	X	X

The three GMFs were further validated with software industry practitioners across the globe. The response from 82 industry practitioners shown below in figure 17 validated the claim that GQM is the preferred model of the three goal measurement frameworks.

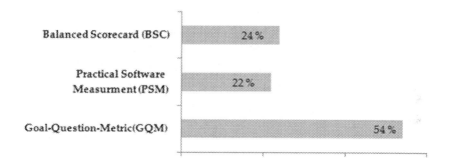

Figure 17: GMFs Validation with software industry practitioners

The table and survey show that GQM is the most suitable model for software project management as it aligns with the organizational goals given that goals shape the targets for measurement, questions support the accomplishment of the goals and metrics provide answers to the questions. According to Berander and Jönsson, GQM is the de-facto standard for the definition of software measurement frameworks [Berander and Jönsson, 2006]. However while the traditional GQM is based on the organization's goals the scope of this research is on the needs of the stakeholders in software projects. Hence the GQM principles were adopted and conscious effort was made to address those limitations especially the ones listed in the literature review chapter while deriving the software project measures

3.4.2 Step 2: Derivation of the Measurement Model

In this phase a stakeholder driven measurement model was built in six steps using the GQM framework.

Step 1: Conduct Stakeholder Analysis

Step 1 is categorizing the stakeholders and identifying the stakeholders' criteria or value propositions for project success. Stakeholder analysis is often considered the first step in strategic planning activities on an organizational level as it helps in understanding the attributes, interrelationships and interfaces between different project elements in strategically planning the project [Smith, 2000]. According to PMBOK, the project management team must identify the stakeholders, determine what their needs and expectations are and then manage and influence those expectations to ensure a successful project [PMI, 2008]. Categorizing the stakeholders also meets the fundamental step in measurement – classification. A proper analysis and classification of the stakeholders will help to understand the right players, their importance in the project, their needs and communication strategies. Moreover as measurement data is expensive to collect, report, and analyze it was essential to identify the stakeholders and their competing demands so that every measure has a customer who will use it.

In this scenario, based on the work of Turner et al [Turner et al, 2009], there are three generic categories of project stakeholders – initiators, implementers and beneficiaries. This classification is also in line with the three different types of stakeholders i.e. owner, customer and user proposed by Peter Jackson [Jackson, 2009]. Table 9 below summarizes the three project stakeholders and their value propositions for project success. The terms within braces in the primary concerns and secondary concerns column are the IS success criteria factors of Delone and Mclean which was explained in the literature review chapter.

Table 9: Project Stakeholder Value Propositions

Stakeholder Group	Typical Software Project Members	Primary Concerns	Secondary Concerns
Initiators	• Project Sponsor • Senior Management	Adherence to Schedule and Cost (Net benefits)	Scope (Intended Use)
Implementers	• Project Manager • Business Analysts • Developers • Tester	Scope/Size (Intended Use)	Adherence to Schedule and Cost (Net benefits)
Beneficiaries	• Product Champion • Super Users • End Users	Quality (System Quality, Information Quality and Service Quality)	Scope/Features (Intended Use)

1. **Initiators.** This group includes stakeholders such as project sponsor, management team et cetera who bring the project into existence. All projects have initiators— typically the business champions who see a need for change, provide resources, and have the authority to make something happen. Without them, the project would not have been proposed or started or existed.

2. **Implementers.** This group includes stakeholders such as the project manager, business analysts, developers and testers including the suppliers who build or execute the project. They translate the project visions and plans into reality through scoping, translating needs into reality, model, and document requirements, build the application, verify, validate, and deploy the application et cetera.

3. **Beneficiaries.** This group is the actual users of the software application. They are usually not interested in how the software works or is implemented. But they desire a functional, reliable, user-friendly and a secure software application.

Step 2: Formulate the Stakeholders Goal (s)

While the stakeholders' needs are normally stated as business goals, the goals from the GQM perspective are the measurement goals. In this step, a generic goal statement from the stakeholder perspective is constructed by applying the goal template in GQM with five dimensions namely: object, purpose, focus, viewpoint and environment.

1. **Object** is an entity that will be measured and analyzed.
2. The **purpose** expresses what will be measured in the object. It is the motivation behind the goal i.e. the "why" the goal exists. It is the reason to achieve the goal.
3. The **focus** is the particular attribute of the object that will be analyzed in the measurement framework.
4. The **viewpoint** provides information about the people who will interpret and use the metrics.
5. Finally, the **environment** is the context in which the measurement study will be performed.

The measurement goal statement encompassing the five dimensions of the GQM framework for a software project will be — "track the **software project** objectively to **deliver the scope** successfully with respect to **size, schedule, cost, and quality (IS critical factors of Delone and Mclean)** from the viewpoint of the **stakeholders** given the high failure in software projects because of a **lack of management visibility during the project duration**".

Step 3: Translate the Goals to Quantifiable Questions

Moving from measurement goals to quantifiable questions is a crucial phase in the GQM model. The entity-question list is the recommended tool to help identify and frame quantifiable questions [Park et al, 1996]. To translate the business or measurement goals of the stakeholder to quantifiable questions, the software project was decomposed into three sub-entities i.e. product, process and resources.

On the product sub-entity, the Zachman's Framework (ZF) was applied. The traditional 6X6 ZF matrix is adapted on the three groups of stakeholders to form a 3X6 matrix. ZF was selected (over The Open Group Architecture Framework - TOGAF and Federal Enterprise Architecture - FEA) for two main reasons.

1. ZF expresses the software product in terms of the needs of the stakeholders'.
2. One of the limitations of GQM is that it does not provide guidance on when to terminate formulating the questions. ZF expresses the needs of the stakeholders' thereby providing a framework for articulating the questions.

Similarly on the process sub-entity, the nine knowledge areas from PMBOK [PMI, 2008] were applied on the three groups of stakeholders. On the resources sub-entity, the five resource dimensions were applied. The questions derived from these three areas i.e. product, process and resources were also mapped to the five project phases – initiation, planning, monitoring, controlling and closure to ensure that all questions pertinent to the project phases are also covered. From this exercise, 204 baseline questions were derived. The list of 204 questions is listed in Appendix 1. The complete application on the three groups of stakeholders is based on the template shown below in table 10 where the indicators A1, A2, ..., T3 indicate the cluster of questions pertaining to the respective project sub-entity.

Table 10: Baseline Question Formulation

Project Sub Entities	Dimensions	Initiator	Implementer	Beneficiary
Product	Data	A1	A2	A3
	Function	B1	B2	B3
	Network	C1	C2	C3
	People	D1	D2	D3
	Time	E1	E2	E3
	Motivation	F1	F2	F3

Process	Integration Management	G1	G2	G3
	Scope Management	H1	H2	H3
	Time Management	I1	I2	I3
	Cost Management	J1	J2	J3
	Quality Management	K1	K2	K3
	Human Resource Management	L1	L2	L3
	Communications Management	M1	M2	M3
	Risk Management	N1	N2	N3
	Procurement Management	O1	O2	O3
Resources	People	P1	P2	P3
	Software	Q1	Q2	Q3
	Supporting Hardware	R1	R2	R3
	Communications Infrastructure	S1	S2	S3
	Facilities	T1	T2	T3

The list of 204 questions was further pruned using the three-by-three importance matrix of **impact** and **influence** on the software project outcome. The nine-blocker is as shown in the figure 18 below. Five stakeholders (a sponsor, a project manager, a developer, a tester and a user) were then asked to categorize the 204 questions into the nine 9 blocks. Questions which were high in influence and impact i.e. the upper-right hand quadrant from all five respondents were considered to be of highest importance for the stakeholders and taken as the baseline questions.

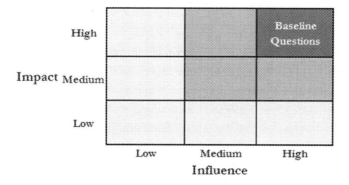

Figure 18: Pruning the Baseline Questions

After further deliberations and analysis between the above five stakeholders, a list of 21 baseline questions was finalized. The 21 questions are:

1. Who are the users of the software application?
2. What is the overall project delivery status?
3. What is the functionality to be delivered?
4. When is the product ready for deployment?
5. Why is the product complex?
6. Where is the impact of changes?
7. How stable are the requirements?
8. What is the critical path?
9. What is the project scope?
10. What factors are critical to quality (CTQ)?
11. When is the project delivery due?
12. What are the risks?
13. Where can the CTQ items be optimized?
14. How much is the budget?
15. How is the current level of quality?
16. Who are the project stakeholders?
17. What kind of skills/resources do we need?
18. What is the project effort and duration?
19. What are the constraints, assumptions and dependencies?
20. How long will the contingency/buffer last?
21. How is the waste in the project determined and addressed?

Getting the right level of abstraction in the questions can be challenging. If questions are too abstract, the relationship between the measure and the question may be muddied. If they are too detailed, it becomes more difficult to get a clear interpretation of the goal. So for getting a complete list of questions further refinement (such as duplication, rewording et cetera) was carried out and 14 questions stakeholders can have in a project were identified. The 14 questions are:

1. How to estimate the size of the project before development?
2. How to know the functional size or size of the project after development?
3. What is total estimated effort? Or how much will this project cost?
4. What is the complexity of the deliverables?
5. What is the estimated duration of this project?
6. What is the current stage of the project?
7. What is the productivity or what are the schedule and effort variances?
8. What is the delivery effectiveness in the project?
9. What is the critical path?
10. What is the current level of quality?
11. What is the impact and amount of re-work/cost of quality?
12. How is the requirements volatility?
13. What is the mean time to failure (MTTF) or what is the process stability?
14. What are the risk levels with respect to schedule, cost and quality?

Step 4: Prioritize the Questions with PCA

The above 14 questions identified were prioritized by a sample set of stakeholders using the Paired Comparison Analysis (PCA) technique to work out the importance of every question relative to each other. This technique helps to set priorities to solve important problems in the absence of historical data. The objective of PCA is twin-fold.

1. To prioritize the 14 questions.
2. Explore if any of these 14 questions can be eliminated.

Fifteen stakeholders – three initiators, seven implementers and five beneficiaries were selected from different companies and from different countries and were asked to give the importance of the 14 questions relative to each other by giving a score from 0 (no difference) to 3 (major difference). From those 15 tables, the final value in each cell was selected based on the common responses. For example, in Q4 v/s Q7 comparison, eleven of the 15 stakeholders had marked Q7 as more important than Q4 and the average score difference between Q4 and Q7 after rounding to the nearest integer was 2 giving the final cell value as (7, 2). The first co-ordinate is the question preferred and the second co-ordinate is the preference score. This exercise was conducted for all the cells and the final values are shown in the table 11 below.

Table 11: Summarized Data from Paired Comparison Analysis (PCA)

(NA – Not Applicable; ND – No Difference; DP - Duplicate)

	Q1	Q2	Q3	Q4	Q5	Q6	Q7	Q8	Q9	Q10	Q11	Q12	Q13	Q14
Q1	NA	ND	1,1	1,2	1,1	6,2	1,1	8,2	1,3	1,2	1,1	1,3	1,2	14,2
Q2	DP	NA	2,1	ND	2,2	6,2	2,1	2,2	2,2	10,2	11,2	2,3	13,2	14,1
Q3	DP	DP	NA	ND	3,1	6,3	7,3	3,1	3,3	3,1	3,2	3,3	3,3	3,2
Q4	DP	DP	DP	NA	4,1	4,2	7,2	4,2	9,3	4,3	4,1	4,2	4,2	14,3
Q5	DP	DP	DP	DP	NA	5,2	5,2	5,1	5,3	10,2	11,2	5,3	13,2	5,2
Q6	DP	DP	DP	DP	DP	NA	6,1	6,2	6,3	10,2	6,2	6,1	13,3	14,2
Q7	DP	DP	DP	DP	DP	DP	NA	8,1	7,3	7,1	11,1	7,2	7,2	7,1
Q8	DP	DP	DP	DP	DP	DP	DP	NA	8,3	8,2	8,1	8,3	8,1	ND
Q9	DP	DP	DP	DP	DP	DP	DP	DP	NA	10,3	ND	9,1	ND	14,3
Q10	DP	DP	DP	DP	DP	DP	DP	DP	DP	NA	10,2	10,2	13,3	10,1
Q11	DP	DP	DP	DP	DP	DP	DP	DP	DP	DP	NA	11,2	11,2	11,3
Q12	DP	DP	DP	DP	DP	DP	DP	DP	DP	DP	DP	NA	12,2	14,2
Q13	DP	DP	DP	DP	DP	DP	DP	DP	DP	DP	DP	DP	NA	13,2
Q14	DP	DP	DP	DP	DP	DP	DP	DP	DP	DP	DP	DP	DP	NA

After adding up all the values for the 14 questions and converting each into a percentage of the total value of preferences i.e.166, we get the preference total for each of the 14 questions as shown below.

- Q1 = 16 (9.9%)
- Q2 = 14 (8.5%)
- Q3 = 16 (9.9%)
- Q4 = 13 (7.8%)
- Q5 = 13 (7.8%)
- Q6 = 16 (9.9%)
- Q7 = 13 (7.8%)
- Q8 = 12(7.3%)
- Q9 = 1 (0.6%)
- Q10 = 14 (8.4%)
- Q11 = 12 (7.3%)
- Q12 = 1 (0.6%)
- Q13 = 12 (7.3%)
- Q14 = 13 (7.8%)

The outcome from PCA indicates that Q9 (What is the critical path?) and Q12 (How is the requirements volatility?) are not accepted by this set of stakeholders. Upon close analysis these two questions were "camouflaged" in the remaining 12 questions. For instance, Q9 on critical path (tasks that determine the end date in the project) was similar to Q5 on project duration. Q12 on requirements volatility in essence questions the impact of schedule, cost and quality in the project and is covered on questions pertaining to questions on risk levels and productivity. So 12 questions to know the project status that were finally selected were:

1. How to estimate the functional size? Or size of the project before development?
2. How to know the size of the project after development?
3. What is total estimated effort? Or how much will this project cost?
4. What is the complexity of the deliverables?
5. What is the estimated duration of this project?

6. What is the current stage of the project?
7. What is the productivity? Or what are the schedule and effort variances?
8. What is the delivery effectiveness in the project?
9. What is the current level of quality?
10. What are the impact /amount of re-work/cost of quality?
11. What is the mean time to failure (MTTF) or process stability?
12. What are the risk levels with respect to schedule, cost and quality?

Step 5: Derive Attributes from the Questions

An attribute is defined as a feature or property of an entity [Fenton and Pfleeger, 1997]. The 12 questions were mapped to the respective project attributes as any measure π is a three-tuple $\prod = (\alpha, \Omega, \mu)$ where, α = Attribute to be measured, Ω = measurement scale, and μ = unit of measure [Wang, 2003]. The six attributes coming out from the 12 questions are:

- Size (physical and functional)
- Complexity (or Maintenance)
- Cost
- Schedule
- Stability (of process and product)
- Quality Achieving Velocity

Stability (of the process and product) and the Quality Achieving Velocity were combined into one attribute group - quality. This step provided five attributes namely **size, complexity, cost, schedule and quality** and ensures that questions can be traced back to the measurement goal through attributes or focus which was one of the dimensions in the formulation of measurement goals.

Step 6: Derive Measures from the Attributes

In GQM, the term metric is loosely defined; it can mean a base measure, a derived measure or a composite of measures. Given that there are hundreds of measures available, five important factors were considered while associating the question (with the attribute) in the selection of appropriate measures.

1. **Application at all phases of the SDLC.**

   Measures selected could be applied in all the SDLC phases (i.e. requirement elicitation, design, development/coding, testing and deployment). Focusing on the entire SDLC, rather than just on one phase, gives a comprehensive knowledge needed to enhance software quality. According to Tom DeMarco, "If you measure exactly the work of design, for instance, and then don't measure the coding at all, people will soon catch on. Their conscious or unconscious reaction will be to push as much of the work as possible into the unmeasured activity" [DeMarco, 1986].

2. **Objectivity.**

   Objective measures are preferred over subjective measures as they bring consistency in the measurement process. As per ISO 15939, objective measures typically provide more accuracy and repeatability than subjective methods and where possible, objective methods of measurement are preferable. An objective measure gives little scope for human judgment in the measurement value. This brings consistency in the measurement process as an objective measure can be measured several times and the same value can be obtained within the measurement error.

3. **Level of Measurement/Scale types.**

   The ratio and interval measures have the highest level of information were preferred over others. Conversely the scale type of the objective measures are either interval or ratio scale [Wohlin et al, 2000]

4. **Availability in existing tools.**

A measure that is already proven i.e. well researched, validated and implemented in tools such as Visual studio, Eclipse and Microsoft Project is selected over others for:

- Easier and quicker implementation,
- Cost effectiveness

5. **Flexibility in Implementation.**

The measures identified should be flexible enough given that refinement and adaptation would be needed during implementation. The two main flexibility factors (FF) are:

- FF1: Derivation/calculation of the measures in more than one way.
    1. FF1 is low (score is 1) if the measure has only one way of determination
    2. FF2 is high (score is 2) if the measure has only more than one way of getting determined.
- FF2: Measurement value available on demand at any stage in the project.
    1. FF2 is low (score is 1) if the measurement value takes more than eight business hours to calculate (assumption is that the relevant data is available) for the control account in the WBS where the project is tracked.
    2. FF2 is high (score is 2) if the measurement value takes less than eight business hours to calculate for the lowest element in the WBS where the project is tracked.

From the above five criteria described the answers to the 12 questions and five attributes came from eight measures namely:

1. **Lines of Code (LOC).**

It is the "physical" count of any programming statement without the blank or comment line [Wolverton, 1974].

2. **Function Points (FP).**

It is the unit of measurement to express the amount of business functionality provided to the business user [Albrecht, 1979].

3. **McCabe's Cyclomatic Complexity (v (G)).**

It measures the technical or system complexity by counting the available decision paths in the program [McCabe, 1976].

While LOC and FP reflect the size of the product, v (G) is indicates the technical complexity of the product or application.

The software project schedule and cost attributes/measures come from earned value management (EVM). EVM measures the project progress in an objective manner combining measurements of scope, schedule, and cost in a single integrated system [Fleming and Koppelman, 2000]. The two measures from EVM are:

4. **Schedule Performance Index (SPI).**

It is an index showing the efficiency of the time utilized in the project. SPI indicates how much ahead or behind schedule the project is [Fleming and Koppelman, 2000].

5. **Cost Performance Index (CPI).**

It shows the efficiency of the utilization of the resources/budget in the project. CPI indicates how much over or under budget the project is [Fleming and Koppelman, 2000].

Quality in the project can be achieved and improved by identifying and resolving the defects. As software quality is a multi-dimensional notion, three measures on quality are selected to address the relevant questions.

6. **Sigma Level (Cpk).**

This indicates the effectiveness or stability of the entire software project delivery process [Pyzdek, 2000]. A higher Cpk indicates a process that is less prone to defects enabling us to achieve repeatable results.

7. Defect Density (DD).

It compares the number of defects in various software components reflecting the stability of different components. It is the ratio of the number of open defects to the size of the software component.

8. Defect Removal Efficiency (DRE).

It indicates the velocity at which quality is achieved i.e. the rate at which defects are resolved.

Appendix 3 explains each of the eight measures in detail. The application of the five criteria in deriving the eight measures is as shown in table 12.

Table 12: Application of the five criteria on the eight measures

SL #	Measure\Criteria	SDLC Phases				Measure Type	Scale Type	Availability in Commercial Tools	Flexibility		
		Req	Design	Dev	Testing				FF1	FF2	FFavg
1	Lines of Code	NA	X	X	X	Objective	Ratio	Development Editors	2	2	2.0
2	Function Points	X	X	X	X	Objective	Ratio	Development Editors	2	2	2.0
3	McCabe's Cyclomatic Complexity	X	X	X	X	Objective	Interval	Development Editors	2	2	2.0
4	SPI	X	X	X	X	Objective	Ratio	Project Mngt Software	1	2	1.5
5	CPI	X	X	X	X	Objective	Ratio	Project Mngt Software	1	2	1.5
6	Sigma Level	X	X	X	X	Objective	Ratio	NA. Manual Calculation	1	2	1.5
7	Defect Density	X	X	X	X	Objective	Ratio	NA. Manual Calculation	1	2	1.5
8	Defect Removal Efficiency (DRE)	X	X	X	X	Objective	Ratio	NA. Manual Calculation	1	2	1.5

Note: Lines of Code (LOC) can be derived indirectly from Function points (FP) and the programing language used in the development. This means using FP the LOC can be estimated even before development in the design phase. David Longstreet has done extensive work in this areas and this is not in scope of this research.

The application of the six steps with the appropriate traceability is as shown below in figure 19.

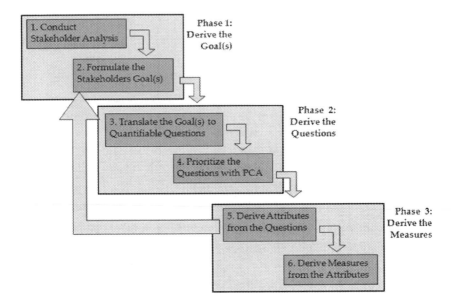

Figure 19: The Six Steps in GQM

Once the eight measures were selected, a reverse GQM or MQG (Metric-Question-Goal) was carried out to ensure that the measures answer the questions and align to the stakeholder needs. This step is needed because some researchers have argued that the top-down approach ignores what is feasible to measure at the bottom and encourage a bottom-up approach, where organizations measure what is available, regardless of goals [Bache and Neil, 1995; Hetzel, 1993].

These eight measures can be classified into three categories. LOC, FP and V (g) fall under product measures. CPI and SPI are the process or resource measures while Cpk, DD and DRE are the quality measures. While LOC, FP, V (g) are base measures CPI, SPI, Cpk, DD and DRE are the derived measures. The application of the generic GQM framework for the three categories of software project stakeholders is as shown below in figure 20. Appendix 2 explains each of the eight measures in detail.

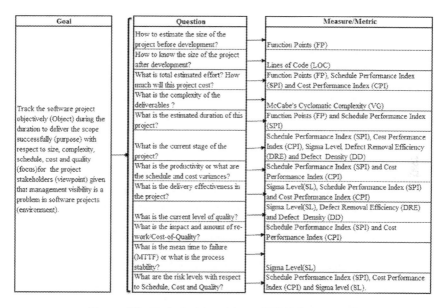

Figure 20: Stakeholder driven GQM framework

3.4.3 Step 3: Derivation of the Validation Criteria

The identification of the validation criteria encompasses – both theoretical and empirical validation criteria. In the absence of generalized and accepted validation criteria, the process followed by Meneely et al was adopted to find the theoretical and empirical validation criteria [Meneely et al, 2010]. Meneely et al carried out a systematic literature review of 2,288 peer-reviewed papers pertaining to software metrics validation and ultimately extracted 47 unique validation criteria from 20 papers as shown in table 13 below.

Table 13: List of all 47 validation criteria
[List adopted from Meneely et al, 2010]

1. A priori validity	25. Monotonicity
2. Actionability	26. Metric Reliability
3. Appropriate Continuity	27. Non-collinearity
4. Appropriate Granularity	28. Non-exploitability
5. Association	29. Non-uniformity
6. Attribute validity	30. Notation validity
7. Causal model validity	31. Permutation validity
8. Causal relationship validity	32. Predictability
9. Content validity	33. Prediction system validity
10. Construct validity	34. Process or Product Relevance
11. Constructiveness	35. Protocol validity
12. Definition validity	36. Rank Consistency
13. Discriminative power	37. Renaming insensitivity
14. Dimensional consistency	38. Repeatability
15. Economic productivity	39. Representation condition
16. Empirical validity	40. Scale validity
17. External validity	41. Stability
18. Factor independence	42. Theoretical validity
19. Improvement validity	43. Trackability
20. Instrument validity	44. Transformation invariance
21. Increasing growth validity	45. Underlying theory validity
22. Interaction sensitivity	46. Unit validity
23. Internal consistency	47. Usability
24. Internal validity	

According to Meneely et al, the list of 47 validation criteria was meant to be a reference. To reduce the list to a more manageable level, papers which were published in the last 20 years and had citations of over 150 in Google scholar was selected. This provided concurrency and relevancy of the research papers and this in turn provided a list of top 6 papers as shown below in table 14. These six papers were cross referenced with the remaining 14 papers to ensure that nothing was left out. These 6 papers were in the cross referencing list identified by Meneely and his team.

Table 14: Top Six Software Metrics Validation Criteria Papers

SL #	Author_Year	Name of the Paper	# of Citations as on July 8th 2012
1	WEYUK1988	Evaluating Software Complexity Measures	587
2	FENTO1994	Software Measurement: A Necessary Scientific Basis	483
3	KITCH1995	Towards a Framework for Software Measurement Validation	447
4	SCHNE1992	Methodology for Validating Software Metrics	315
5	FENTO2000	Software Metrics: Roadmap	225
6	BRAIN1996	On the application of Measurement Theory in Software Engineering	153

The validation criteria list from these 6 papers came down to 28 from 47 and these criteria are as shown in table 15 below.

Table 15: List of 28 validation criteria

SL #	Criteria	WEYUK1988	SCHNE1992	FENTO1994	KITCH1995	BRAIN1996	FENTO2000
1	A priori validity			Y		Y	
2	Actionability						Y
3	Appropriate Continuity				Y		
4	Appropriate Granularity	Y			Y		
5	Association		Y	Y			
6	Attribute Validity				Y		
7	Causal Model Validity						Y
8	Discriminative Power		Y				
9	Dimensional Consistency				Y		
10	External Validity			Y		Y	
11	Instrument Validity				Y		
12	Increasing growth Validity	Y					
13	Interaction Sensitivity	Y					
14	Monotonicity	Y					
15	Non-Uniformity	Y					
16	Permutation Validity	Y					
17	Predictability		Y	Y			
18	Process/Product Relevance		Y				
19	Protocol Validity				Y		
20	Rank Consistency		Y				
21	Renaming Insensitivity	Y					
22	Repeatability		Y				
23	Representation Condition			Y	Y		
24	Scale Validity			Y	Y		
25	Theoritical Validity			Y		Y	
26	Trackability		Y				
27	Underlying Theory Validity				Y		
28	Unit Validity			Y	Y		

To further prune the list, each of the papers was studied in detail. Though, Weyuker's paper was in the above table 15 i.e. WEYUK1998, it was decided to not include Weyuker's validation criteria for the following reasons:

1. Her criteria have been intensely contested by other metrics validation researchers over the years and many are found to be weak [Meneely et al, 2010].

2. Her validation criteria are closely related to the representation condition, a property that many researchers cite as the most important category in metrics validation. Representation Condition criterion will however be covered as part of the work done by Kitchenham et al [Kitchenham et al, 1995].

So six of the seven criteria proposed by Weyuker were dropped as it appeared only in her paper. The seventh criteria i.e. Appropriate Granularity was included because it appeared in KITCH1995. Then the two lowest cited papers i.e. BRAIN1996 and FENTO2000 were studied to look for any opportunities to reduce the list.

From the paper BRAIN1996 i.e. "On the Application of Measurement Theory in Software Engineering", the validation criteria included:

1. A Priori Validity
2. External Validity
3. Theoretical Validity

From the paper FENTO2000 i.e. "Software Metrics: Roadmap", the validation criteria included:

1. Action-ability
2. Causal Model Validity

• **A Priori Validity** criterion was mentioned in both BRAIN1996 and FENTO1994 as shown in table 10. A metric has a priori validity if the attributes in association are specified in advance of finding a correlation. This is closely related to the Association criterion mentioned as part of the empirical validation criteria by Schneidewind i.e. SCHNE1992. So "A Priori Validity" criterion will be dropped for Association criterion.

- As said in section 2.3, **External validity** is also known as empirical validity. External/Empirical validation itself is a broad category of validation and it is related to some way with an external factor [El Emam, 2000]. Hence we drop this criterion from the list due to its abstractness. In addition, all of Schneidewind's six validation criteria in SCHNE1992 fall under empirical validation.

- As mentioned earlier, **theoretical/internal validation** is a broad category of validation and it is related to measurement theory axioms. Hence we drop this criterion from the list due to its abstractness.

- **Actionability** which appears in FENTO1004 allows for making empirically informed decisions. We will drop this for Schneidewind's empirical validation criteria list.

- **Causal Model Validity** is used to explain an external factor which belongs to External/Empirical validation. We will drop this for Schneidewind's empirical validation criteria list.

So these five criteria (from BRAIN1996 and FENTO2000) were also dropped along with the six dropped earlier from Weyuker. This brings the list of criteria to 17 (17 = 28 - 6 − 5) from three papers. The list of 17 validation criteria is as shown in the table 16 below.

Table 16: List of 17 Validation Criteria

SL #	Criteria	SCHNE1992	FENTO1994	KITCH1995
1	Appropriate Continuity			Y
2	Appropriate Granularity			Y
3	Association	Y	Y	
4	Attrubute Validity			Y
5	Discriminative Power	Y		
6	Dimensional Consistency			Y
7	Instrument Validity			Y
8	Predictability	Y	Y	
9	Process/Product Relevance	Y		
10	Protocol Validity			Y
11	Rank Consistency	Y		
12	Repeatability	Y		
13	Representation Condition		Y	Y
14	Scale Validity		Y	Y
15	Trackability	Y		
16	Underlying Theory Validity			Y
17	Unit Validity		Y	Y

Each of the 17 criteria was again studied thoroughly to see if any of the criteria can be dropped.

- Criterion # 9 in table 11 i.e. Process/Product Relevance from SCHNE1992 refers to the tailoring of the metric to specific products or processes. This criterion is not applicable as the goal of this research is to derive metric/measure for the software project and not for specific products or processes.

- Criterion #11 i.e. A metric has **rank consistency** if it shares the same ranking as a quality factor [Schneidewind 1991]. The rank consistency validation is very similar to the definition of association which states that "a metric has **association validity** if it has a direct, linear statistical correlation with an external quality factor [Schneidewind 1991]". Hence to prevent duplication, rank consistency is dropped from the list.

- Criterion # 16 i.e. Underlying Theory Validity is associated with internal/theoretical and external/empirical validity [Kitchenham et al, 1995]. As external/empirical validity is a broad category of validation and it is related to some way with an external factor [El Emam, 2000], we drop this criterion from the list due to its abstractness.

This brings the total list of validity criteria to 14. The 14 criteria came from the works from the works of Kitchenham, Schneidewind and Fenton. These 14 criteria were categorized into seven theoretical and seven empirical validity criteria. The final list of 14 criteria is as shown in table 17 below. The detailed explanations of these validation criteria is explained in Appendix 3.

Table 17: List of Final 14 Validation Criteria

SL #	Criteria	Type	SCH92	FEN94	KIT95
1	Appropriate Continuity	Theoretical			Y
2	Appropriate Granularity	Theoretical			Y
3	Association	Empirical	Y	Y	
4	Attribute Validity	Empirical			Y
5	Discriminative Power	Empirical	Y		
6	Dimensional Consistency	Theoretical			Y
7	Instrument Validity	Empirical			Y
8	Predictability	Empirical	Y	Y	
9	Protocol Validity	Theoretical			Y
10	Repeatability	Empirical	Y		
11	Representation Condition	Theoretical		Y	Y
12	Scale Validity	Theoretical		Y	Y
13	Trackability	Empirical	Y		
14	Unit Validity	Theoretical		Y	Y

3.4.4 Step 4: Validation

According to Braind, Khaled and Sandro both theoretical and empirical validation must be carried out to avoid the problem of defining a theoretically sound measure which is otherwise useless in its practical application [Braind, Khaled and Sandro, 1995]. Given the fact that greater the evidence the more valid is the measure, the validation of the measurement model includes both theoretical and empirical validation.

3.4.4.1 Theoretical Validation

In addition, to applying the seven theoretical validation criteria the ten questions of Kaner and Bond were also applied on the measurement model to ensure that it works successfully during empirical validation [Kaner and Bond, 2004]. The ten questions of Kaner and Bond were:

1. What is the purpose of this measure?
2. What is the scope of this measure?
3. What is the natural scale for the measure?
4. What attribute measured?
5. What is the natural scale of the attribute measured?
6. What is the natural variability of the attribute?
7. What is the relationship of the attribute to the measured value?
8. What measuring instrument is used to perform the measurement?
9. What is the natural variability of readings from the instrument?
10. What are the natural and foreseeable side effects of using this instrument?

3.4.4.2 Empirical Validation

As mentioned in research design, empirical validation was carried out on the seven criteria and mixed research methodology; quantitative research with survey and qualitative research with case study. While each of the seven validation criteria will be applicable for both case study and survey, for better management the seven empirical validation criteria are mapped to the two research methods i.e. survey and case studies as shown in the below table 18.

Table 18: Empirical Validation Criteria

#	Empirical Validation Criteria	Research Method
1	Association	Survey
2	Attribute Validity	Survey
3	Discriminative Power	Case Study
4	Instrument Validity	Case study
5	Predictability	Survey
6	Repeatability	Survey
7	Trackability	Case Study

As mentioned in the literature review chapter, one of the important drawbacks of GQM is that it does not bring uniqueness in the measurement model for the same goal(s) and questions of the stakeholders. To address this issue qualitative method (with case studies) and quantitative method (with survey) was needed to identify if there are any measures that need to be included in the measurement model. As empirical validation has a significant portion of research, the case studies and survey design will be covered in separate sections i.e. in sections 3.5 and 3.6.

3.5 Empirical Validation with Case studies

A case study is an in-depth investigation of a single individual, group, or event to find underlying principles within a specific time space. Case studies provide a systematic way of understanding why a particular instance happened and what might become important to look more extensively for future research [Yin, 2009]. In addition, the case study is carried out to:

- Validate the measurement model for the three empirical validation criteria namely - discriminative power, instrument validity and Trackability.

- Ensure that the implementation challenges in the measurement model are addressed.

The case study was applied before the survey as it was essential to see if the measurement model can be implemented in a real world setting to critically examine the issues in the implementation and validation of the measurement model. Moreover case study was applied first to get close to the phenomena and discover causal links, motivations, reasons, why things happened et cetera because in deriving the implementation of the quantitative research i.e. survey questionnaire is clean, complete, and correct so that useful data can be collected in the survey.

The key element in the case study that needed operational definition for the research question RQ1 is the term **"objective project status"** for the three groups of stakeholder namely i.e. initiators, implementers and beneficiaries. When the stakeholder analysis done while deriving the GQM model (in step 1), for initiators and implementers the accurate and objective decision criteria was based on the cost and schedule and for beneficiaries the decision criteria was based on quality.

1. **For Initiators and Implementers**

   +/- 10% of the cost and duration between the baselined project plan and the final cost and duration [Humphrey, 2005]. This was applied on the SPI and CPI measures.

2. **For Beneficiaries**

   To address the success criteria of the beneficiaries, the below two criteria were applied on Cpk, DD and DRE measures.

   a. **Defect rate according to CMMI levels.**

   While the measure "Defect rate" is not one of the eight measures in the measurement model, defect rate is basically the defect that is still unresolved at a specific point in time.

In fact all the three quality measures in the measurement model i.e. Cpk, DD and DRE are in fact derived using the defect rates.

In this backdrop, according to Capers Jones, the effective defect rates per function point can range from 0.75 for a CMMI Level 1(Initial) to 0.05 for a CMMI Level 5 (Optimized) project/organization [Kan, 2003].

b. **DRE Levels**

According to David Longstreet, a software project is mature if the DRE is greater than 45% [Longstreet, 2008].

Along with answering the two research questions, the other key questions specific to the case study are:

- **What data are relevant to collect?**

    1. Baselined project schedule and budget data pertaining to the two measures — SPI and CPI.
    2. Agreeing on the appropriate CMMI levels for the project. While the organization might be certified on a specific CMMI level, does the project adhere to that standard?
    3. The actual data on the eight core measures (LOC, FP, v (G), SPI, CPI, Cpk, DD and DRE).

- **How to analyze data?**

    1. The appropriate levels of thresholds, variances and control limits for the eight measures by the stakeholders.

3.6 Empirical Validation with Survey

After the case study was completed out, the survey was deployed to collect the feedback on the measurement model from the software industry practitioners to identify the characteristics of the broad population of individuals. Cross sectional survey was employed without any loaded, leading and double barreled questions. The unit of analysis in the survey was project stakeholders such as sponsor, project manager, business analyst, developer, tester and users to name a few who have worked in hybrid COTS and bespoke software projects. The defining characteristic of the survey is the selection of the representative sample from a well-defined population and data analysis techniques used to generalize from the sample to the population.

The survey was designed on a five point Likert scale where the respondents were asked to evaluate or rank their level of agreement or disagreement on the applicability of the measure in achieving its intended purpose using the five ordered response levels (namely strongly disagree = 1, disagree = 2, neutral = 3, agree = 4, and strongly agree = 5). The responses were treated as ordinal or rank data as they have an inherent order or sequence and one cannot assume that respondents perceive all pairs of adjacent levels as equidistant. For example, one cannot assume that the difference between "agreeing" and "strongly agreeing" is the same as between "agreeing" and being "neutral".

Since survey research was based on a sample of the population, the success of the research is a function of the representativeness of the population of concern. A good sample size (SS) also helps in generalizing the findings using statistical inferential techniques to the entire population. The sample size (SS) is given as:

$$SS = Z^2 * (P) * (1-P) / C^2$$

Where:

- Z = Using a Z-score table, the Z value for 95% **confidence level** is 1.96.
- P = Predict the **proportion** of the study.

- C = **Confidence interval** i.e. margin of error and it is taken as 10%.

To determine the Lower Specification Limit (LSL) of sample size, the participation factor of 0.7 was applied because in the pilot studies conducted during the survey questionnaire design, 70% of the participants had responded to the survey. This gave the sample size a LSL value of 81. To determine the Upper Specification Limit (USL), a 90 % participation in the survey was considered, and this provided the USL of 138. So the survey was targeted between 81 to 138 respondents. In addition quotas, with a minimum of 20 respondents in each of the three stakeholder groups were set to ensure that a sufficient number of respondents from the sampling frame represented all three types of stakeholders.

While the measurement model had eight measures, the survey questionnaire had an additional variable Om, which is the overall measure where the eight core measures in totality can be used to describe the accurate and objective status of the software project. Statistical analysis included tools two major areas:

1. Descriptive Statistics
2. Inferential Statistics

3.6.1 Descriptive Statistics

Descriptive statistics quantitatively describe and summarize a data set. Five main tools will be used to describe the data collected on the eight measures in the survey questionnaire. They are:

1. Stakeholder Profile

   This includes the stakeholder type, geographic distribution, number of years of experience, type of organizations these stakeholders belong to et cetera.

2. Bar charts and Scatter plots and not histograms (as the data is not continuous).

    A bar chart here will be a vertical rectangular bar with lengths proportional to the count of responses of the stakeholders on the five Likert scales.

    The scatter plot will display values of the each of the measures with the overall measure Om. The overall measure Om is the virtual measure where all the eight measures are considered as one holistic measure.

3. Skewness and Kurtosis

    Kurtosis is a measure of whether the data are peaked or flat relative to a normal distribution i.e. data sets with high kurtosis (positive or negative) tend to have a distinct peak near the mean, decline rather rapidly, and have heavy tails. Data sets with low kurtosis tend to have a flat top near the mean rather than a sharp peak.

    Skewness is a measure of the asymmetry of the distribution. The skewness value can be positive or negative, or zero.

4. Central tendency summarized by median (with box plots) and mode and not mean.

    Central tendency relates to the way in which quantitative data is clustered around some value such as mean, median, or other measure of location, depending on the context. In the context of this thesis, as the survey response is of ordinal data type, the "some value" is the median and the Central tendency will be summarized through:

    o Smallest observation (sample minimum),
    o Lower quartile (Q1)
    o Median (Q2)

    ○ Upper quartile (Q3) and

    ○ Largest observation (sample maximum).

5. Variability summarized by range and inter-quartile range and not standard deviation.

Range which provides an indication of statistical dispersion is calculated by subtracting the smallest observation from the greatest.

The inter-quartile range (IQR) is the measure of statistical dispersion, being equal to the difference between the upper and lower quartiles. $IQR = Q_3 - Q_1$

3.6.2 Inferential Statistics

Inferential statistics is used to draw conclusions that extend beyond the sample data collected to infer from the sample data the characteristics of the population. After summarizing and describing the data, the next step is to know whether the findings in the study could be generalized beyond the relatively small number of the sample studied. This is referred to as external validity or generalizability. In this backdrop, four inferential statistical techniques will be used to analyze the survey data. They are:

1. Net Promoter Score (NPS)
2. Pearson's Correlation
3. Regression Analysis
4. Hypothesis Testing on:
    ○ Similar Measures (HM)
    ○ Stakeholder groups (HS)

A. Net Promoter Score (NPS)

The "Net Promote Score (NPS)" technique introduced by Fred Reichheld gives a simple and effective summary of the survey results [Reichheld,2003]. NPS is based on the fundamental perspective that every respondent can be divided into three categories: Promoters, Passives, and Detractors based on their ratings on the Likert scale. Based on the response, survey respondents were categorized as follows:

- Survey respondents who gave score of 4 and 5 were classified as are promoters
- Survey respondents who gave score of 3 are satisfied but neutral
- Survey respondents who gave score of 1 and 2 were grouped as critics

To calculate the Net Promoter Score (NPS), the percentage of respondents who are promoters is taken and subtracted from the percentages who are critics. An NPS efficiency rating between 50% to 80% is considered good [Reichheld, 2003]. The most important benefits of the NPS method is simplifying and communicating the objective of creating more "promoters" and fewer "detractors" — a concept claimed to be far simpler to understand and act on than more complicated, obscure or hard-to-understand satisfaction metrics or indices. In addition, net promoter method can also reduce the complexity of implementation and analysis, and provide a stable measure of performance that can be easily compared.

B. Pearson's Correlation

The Pearson's correlation co-efficient is designated by the letter "r" reflects the degree of linear relationship between two variables. It ranges from +1 to -1. A correlation of +1 means that there is a perfect positive linear relationship between variables and a correlation of -1 means that there is a perfect negative linear relationship between variables. The scatter plot typically depicts the relationship between the variables.

A correlation co-efficient between 0.3 and 0.7 is considered satisfactory; though the values between 0.7 and 1.0 are prefered [Schneidewind, 1992]. In this research thesis, the format for analyzing the Pearson's correlation between each of the eight measures and the overall measure Om is as shown in the table 19 below.

Table 19: Format for Analyzing Pearson's correlation co-efficient

#	Association	Value of r
1	LOC v/s Om	
2	FP v/s Om	
3	V(g) v/s Om	
4	CPI v/s Om	
5	SPI v/s Om	
6	Cpk v/s Om	
7	DD v/s Om	
8	DRE v/s Om	

Once the Pearson's correlation co-efficient is determined, the significance test is conducted to ensure that the correlation is not a chance occurrence. The eight null hypotheses Ho are as shown in table below.

Table 20: Null Hypothesis Statements for Correlation

#	Null Hypothesis Statement
1	There is no association between LOC and Om in the population i.e. r1 = 0
2	There is no association between FP and Om in the population i.e. r2 = 0
3	There is no association between v(G) and Om in the population i.e. r3 = 0
4	There is no association between CPI and Om in the population i.e. r4 = 0
5	There is no association between SPI and Om in the population i.e. r5 = 0
6	There is no association between Cpk and Om in the population i.e. r6 = 0
7	There is no association between DD and Om in the population i.e. r7 = 0
8	There is no association between DRE and Om in the population i.e. r8 = 0

A null hypothesis implies no relationship between independent and dependent variables. If the null hypothesis is rejected, the alternate hypothesis (Ha) will be accepted. Basically the null hypothesis and the alternative hypothesis are complementary. The three pieces of information that will be used for testing the significance of the above eight hypothesis are:

1. The significance level α which is set as 0.05. Significance levels are used to reject the null hypothesis and a significance level of

'0.05' is conventionally used. Setting $\alpha = 0.05$ implies that there is a 5% chance that the strength of the relationship calculated i.e. ρ happened by chance if null hypothesis were true. If the test of significance gives a p-value lower than the significance level α i.e. 0.05, the null hypothesis is rejected. Such results are referred to as 'statistically significant'.

2. The Degree of freedom "DF" which is Ni-2 = 8-2 = 6
3. As there is no prior theory to suggest whether the relationship between each of the eight measures and the overall measure "Om" would be positive or negative, 2-tailed test is adopted to find the critical value using α and DF. This means if the ρ value is greater than the critical value (or less than the negative of the critical value) or P-value is less than α, null hypothesis is rejected.

In this thesis, the value "t" is computed using the following formula:

$$t = \frac{r\sqrt{N-2}}{\sqrt{1-r^2}}$$

Where r is the Pearson's correlation co-efficient and N is the sample size. Once the t-value is determined, we use the two-tail table to compute the p-value.

C. Regression Analysis

Regression analysis helps one understand how the typical value of the dependent variable changes when any one of the independent variables is varied, while the other independent variables are held fixed. The key element in regression analysis there is always one response or dependent variable. In this thesis, the overall measure Om is the dependent variable and the eight measures are the independent variables. A typical regression model will be:

$$Y = Fn\ (Xi,\ X2,...,\ Xn,\ \beta)$$

Where the,

- Dependent variable is, Y.
- Independent variables are X1 to Xn.
- Unknown parameters denoted as β known as residual.

Though there are many regression models, in this thesis three models will be examined. They are:

1. **Multiple Linear Regression**

   In a Multiple Linear Regression model, there will be one predictor and multiple explanatory variables. The general equation for multiple regression model is:

   $Y = a + b_1{}^*X_1 + b_2{}^*X_2 + ... + b_p{}^*X_p$

2. **Polynomial Regression.**

   The assumption that the regression model is linear may not hold. The regression model will be an nth order polynomial such as:

   $$y = a_0 + a_1 x + a_2 x^2 + a_3 x^3 + \cdots + a_m x^m + \varepsilon.$$

3. **Logistic regression**

   Finally as the survey response data is ordinal, the regression models for ordinal data will be developed using Logistic regression. The form of the logistic model formula is:

   P = 1/ (1+exp(-(B0 + B1*X1 + B2*X2 + ... + Bk*Xk)))

   Where B0 is a constant and Bi are coefficients of the predictor variables (or dummy variables in the case of multi-category predictor variables). The computed value, P, is a probability in the range 0 to 1.

In this thesis the regression analysis will be first carried out with Multiple Linear Regression analysis at 95% confidence interval. The residuals, predicted "Y" i.e. Om, the value of goodness-of-fit (the value R^2 is the goodness of fit which is between 0.0 and 1.0), the predicted values with the actual survey results and other parameters will be analyzed. According to Schneidewind if the value of R^2 i.e. goodness of fit is greater than 0.5 the regression model provides a good amount of predictably [Schneidewind, 1991]. Hence if the value of the goodness of fit is greater than 0.50, then the model coming out of Multiple Linear Regression will be adopted. If not Polynomial or logistic Regression methods will be pursued till the goodness-of-fit value is close to 0.50.

The hypothesis testing will be to testing if each of the eight measures is related to the overall measure Om. Specifically the null and alternate hypothesis for each of the eight co-efficient will be:

Ho: $\beta k = 0$
Ha: $\beta k \neq 0$

where k is from 1 to 8 for the eight measures.

D. Other Hypothesis Testing

Two other hypotheses namely D1 and D2 testing will also be applied for further insights on the measurement model. The significance level α and the decision rules are the same that are used in correlation testing.

D1. Relationship between Similar Measures (HM)

This hypothesis testing is to investigate if any of the five "similar" measures have any relationship. Five similar measures were identified based on similarities in the attributes or in the way they were derived. The five "similar" measurement constructs are:

1. LOC and FP (Similarity was because both the measures were associated with the size attribute)

2. SPI and CPI (Similarity was due to way these two measures were derived as they are associated with EVM)
3. Cpk and DD(Similarity of the two measures was due to their association to the Quality attribute)
4. DRE and DD (Similarity of the two measures was due to their association to the Quality attribute)
5. DRE and Cpk(Similarity of the two measures was due to their association to the Quality attribute)

The formulation of the null hypothesis (Ho) which is the hypothesis being tested is as shown below.

1. LOC and FP. The null hypothesis (HM-Ho1) is that there is no association between the LOC and FP measures.
2. SPI and CPI. The null hypothesis (HM-Ho2) is that there is no association between the SPI and CPI measures.
3. Cpk and DD. The null hypothesis (HM-Ho3) is that there is no association between the Cpk and DD measures.
4. DRE and DD. The null hypothesis (HM-Ho4) is that there is no association between the DRE and DD measures.
5. DRE and Cpk. The null hypothesis (HM-Ho5) is that there is no association between the DRE and Cpk measures.

Each of the five hypothesis testing is conducted using Chi-square testing where the null hypothesis Ho assumes that there is no association between the two measures (in other words, one variable does not vary according to the other variable), while the alternative hypothesis Ha claims that some association does exist. The null hypothesis in all the above five cases will be rejected if the p-value will be less than significance level α value of 0.05.

D2. Relationship between the three stakeholders groups (HS)

This hypothesis testing is to investigate if stakeholder's preferences for the measures are similar. This is needed because while formulating the measurement model (step 1 in section 3.4.2), the stakeholder analysis was done based on the measures proposed by

Turner et al. This testing is a validation of those findings. The Kruskal-Wallis (KW) Test tests the null hypothesis that *k* samples from possibly different populations actually originate from similar populations, at least as far as their central tendencies, or medians, are concerned. The test assumes that the variables under consideration have underlying continuous distributions. The KW test was applied on the three stakeholder groups (initiators, implementers and beneficiaries) on the nine measures (eight derived from the GQM model plus the Overall measure Om) with data sets as per the format in the below table 20

Table 21: Format for the application of KW test on the three stakeholder groups

Measures	Initiators	Implementers	Beneficiaries	p-value
LOC				
FP				
V(G)				
CPI				
SPI				
Cpk				
DD				
DRE				
Om				

The formulation of the null hypothesis (Ho) which is the hypothesis being tested is as shown below.

1. HS-Ho1 states that the data coming from initiators, implementers and beneficiaries for FP measure comes from the same population.
2. HS-Ho2 states that the data coming from initiators, implementers and beneficiaries for LOC measure comes from the same population.
3. HS-Ho3 states that the data coming from initiators, implementers and beneficiaries for V(G) measure comes from the same population.

4. HS-Ho4 states that the data coming from initiators, implementers and beneficiaries for CPI measure comes from the same population.

5. HS-Ho5 states that the data coming from initiators, implementers and beneficiaries for SPI measure comes from the same population.

6. HS-Ho6 states that the data coming from initiators, implementers and beneficiaries for Cpk measure comes from the same population.

7. HS-Ho7 states that the data coming from initiators, implementers and beneficiaries for DD measure comes from the same population.

8. HS-Ho8 states that the data coming from initiators, implementers and beneficiaries for DRE measure comes from the same population.

9. HS-Ho9 states that the data coming from initiators, implementers and beneficiaries for Om measure comes from the same population.

The null hypothesis HS-Ho1 to HS-Ho9 state that the k samples for each of the nine measures come from the same population. This means if the null hypothesis is true, then the test statistic, H, used in the KW procedure is greater than the critical value. The test statistic H is defined as follows:

$$H = \frac{12}{N(N+1)} \sum_{i=1}^{k} \frac{R_i^2}{n_i} - 3(N+1)$$

where

- k = number of samples (groups) which in this case is the three stakeholder groups namely initiators, implementers and beneficiaries.
- n_i = number of observations for the i-th sample or group.
- N = total number of observations (sum of all the n_i)
- R_i = sum of ranks for group i

In this case there will be nine values of H for the nine measures. If the critical value for $\alpha = .05$ with $df = k-1 = 3-1 = 2$ is X. If the Hi > X, we reject the null hypothesis concluding that the samples come from the different population. In terms of the p-value, the null hypothesis will be rejected if the p-value will be less than α value of 0.05.

The complete hypothesis framework (Correlation, similar measures i.e HM and stakeholder groups i.e. HS) is as shown in the figure 22 below. The "bold lines" indicates correlation while the "dotted lines" are used to test the hypothesis between similar measures and to investigate if there is any relationship between them.

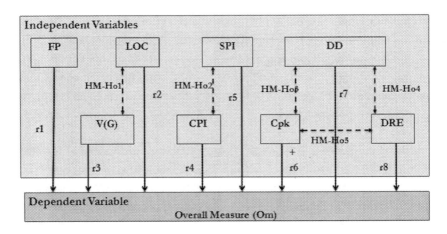

Figure 22: The Hypothesis Framework

3.7 Reliability of Empirical Validation

Closely associated with empirical validity is reliability. Reliability is the consistency of the scores of a test (while validity is the degree of accuracy of the measurement done). The key point in reliability is that it is estimated. In this research thesis, the reliability tests are conducted for three elements — survey questionnaire, survey response data and case study.

1. **Reliability of the survey questionnaire**

The two reliability tests that are applied on the survey questionnaire are:

a. **Test-Retest Reliability Test**

Test-Retest is one of the simplest ways of testing the reliability of an "instrument" over time and assumes that there will be no change in the quality or construct being measured. The idea behind Test-Retest is that one should get the same score on test 1 and test 2. The three main steps in this method are:

1. Run the tests test 1 and test 2 at two separate times for each subject ensuring that there is no change in the underlying conditions between test # 1 and test # 2.
2. Compute the correlation between the two tests i.e. test 1 and test 2.
3. If the correlations between two tests is high (i.e. 0.7 or higher) then there is a good test-retest reliability.

The disadvantage with Test-retest reliability test is the potential for a carryover effect between testing. The first testing may influence the second testing resulting in the contamination of scores. One of ways this effect can however be reduced is by having a sufficient time gap between the two tests.

b. **Cronbach's Internal Consistency test**

In Cronbach's Alpha one split-half reliability is computed and then randomly the items are divided into another set of split halves and re-computed again. This is done until all possible split half estimates of reliability are computed. Essentially, Cronbach's alpha splits all the questions on the measurement instrument in every possible way and computes correlation values for all of them and generate one number known as

Cronbach's alpha. If this value is greater than 0.7, the data set is accepted for reliability [Allen and Yen, 2001].

2. **Reliability of the survey response data**

   The reliability of the data collected from the survey respondents were assessed using the index of variation (IV). Lower the index of variation, lower is the variation and more is the reliability.

3. **Reliability of the case study.**

   To bring reliability in the case study, the three key factors that were considered were:

   • Prolonged and regular data collection process
   • Triangulation
   • Member Checks

The statistical analysis of the survey responses for reliability and validity is as shown in the figure 23 below.

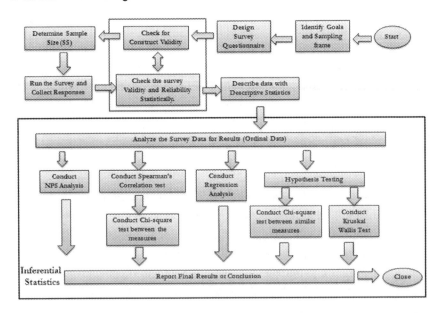

Figure 23: Survey Analysis Flowchart

3.8 Conclusion

The general research paradigm which are characterized through their: ontology, epistemology and methodology was applied on the IS research framework proposed by Henver on the two research questions pertaining to measurement model and its validation. The research paradigm was based on a combination of positivist (objective) and interpretative (subjective) perspectives. The research design leveraged the research paradigm in four stages and the research methodology was then formulated. The application of the methodology using the GQM framework provided the eight measures to track the status of a hybrid and bespoke software projects. In addition fourteen validation criteria – seven theoretical and seven empirical were also identified to validate the measurement model. While deriving the measurement model scientifically is important, validating it is also equally important. Hence validating strategies included both theoretical validation and empirical validation. The empirical validation was mixed methods research – a combination of survey and case studies. Based on the validation criteria, the next chapter looks at the analysis of the theoretical validation and empirical validation strategies for an effective and reliable measurement model.

Chapter 4

Analysis of Research Results

4.1 Introduction

This chapter emphasizes the underlying concepts in describing and analyzing research results. The purpose of this chapter is to summarize the collected data and the statistical treatment, including the mechanics of analysis. Specifically, this chapter applies the 14 validation criteria – seven theoretical and seven empirical on the eight measures. First the theoretical validation is carried out and then the ten questions of Kaner and Bond are applied on the measurement model. In the second part of this chapter, the application the seven empirical validation criteria is applied on case studies and the survey instrument.

4.2 Analysis of Theoretical Validation

As discussed in chapter 3, the measurement model has to be validated theoretically using the seven theoretical validation criteria. In addition the ten questions proposed by Cem Kaner and Walter Bond were applied on the measurement model to ensure a better transition from theoretical to empirical validation [Kaner and Bond, 2004].

4.2.1 Analysis of Seven Theoretical Validation Criteria

According to the research methodology presented in chapter 3, a measure is considered theoretically valid, if it confirms to the seven criteria namely:

1. Scale Validity
2. Appropriate Granularity
3. Representation Condition
4. Unit Validity
5. Protocol Validity
6. Appropriate Continuity
7. Dimensional Consistency

The first five validation criteria namely - Scale Validity, Appropriate Granularity, Representation Condition, Unit Validity and Protocol Validity are relevant for direct or base measures while the two remaining criteria namely Appropriate Continuity and Dimensional Consistency are related to indirect or derived or composite measures as they are derived by mathematical formula involving other measures.

1. Scale Validity

The "Scale Type- Property" relationship on the eight measures of the measurement model is summarized below in table. As the eight measures are either interval or ratio type of measures, only the interval or ratio scales are considered in the table 22 below.

Table 22: Scale Type Property

Sl #	Property	Interval (v(G))	Ratio (other 7 Measures)
1	Equality	Yes	Yes
2	Uniqueness	Yes	Yes
3	Ordinality	Yes	Yes
4	Difference / Interval ratios	Yes	Yes
5	Value Ratios		Yes

2. Appropriate Granularity

As mentioned in Chapter 3, the Granularity of the measure can be fine, medium, and coarse. Of the eight measures in the measurement model, seven of them have fine granularity except for FP. The. The granularity for FP is medium as more granularity can be achieved at the feature level than at the function level. The Appropriate Granularity validity criterion is summarized in the below table 23.

Table 23: Granularity of Measures

Measure	Attribute	Granularity
LOC	Physical program size	Fine
FP	Functional program size	Medium
v(G)	Decision path based program Complexity	Fine
CPI	Variation/Adherence to Budget	Fine
SPI	Variation/Adherence to Schedule	Fine
Cpk	SDLC Process Stability	Fine
DD	Module/Program Code Stability	Fine
DRE	Quality Achieving Velocity	Fine

3. Representation Condition Validity

In the measurement model, LOC satisfies the representation condition for physical program size but it doesn't for functional program size because one can have a poorly written program with more LOC but same or less functionality and vice versa. Hence if the eight measures have to be validated against representation condition, its attributes must be clearly defined. This is done when formulating the 12 questions formulated in chapter 3 while deriving the GQM framework. The application of Representation Condition Validity on the eight measures is as shown in table 24 below.

Table 24: Representation Condition (RC) Validity

Measure	Attribute	RC Validity
LOC	Physical program size; size after development	Yes
FP	Functional program size; size before development	Yes
v(G)	Program Complexity	Yes
CPI	Cost/Budget Performance; Productivity	Yes
SPI	Schedule Performance	Yes
Cpk	Process Stability	Yes
DD	Module Stability	Yes
DRE	Quality Achieving Velocity	Yes

4. Unit Validity

The application of unit validity on the eight measures is as shown in table 25 below.

Table 25: Unit Validity

Measure	Attribute	Definition Model Type	Unit Validity
LOC	Physical program size i.e. size after development	Standard Definition	Yes
FP	Functional program size i.e. size before development	Standard Definition	Yes
v(G)	Program Complexity	Standard Definition	Yes
CPI	Cost/Budget Performance; Productivity	Theoretical Definition	Yes
SPI	Schedule Performance	Theoretical Definition	Yes
Cpk	Process Stability	Theoretical Definition	Yes
DD	Module Stability	Composite Definition	Yes
DRE	Quality Achieving Velocity	Composite Definition	Yes

5. Protocol Validity

The adherence of the eight measures on Protocol Validity is as shown in table 26.

Table 26: Protocol Validity

| Measure | Protocol Validity | | |
	Attribute	Scale	Dimension Analysis
LOC	Physical program size; size after development	Ratio	Dimensionless
FP	Functional program size; size before development	Ratio	Dimensionless
v(G)	Program Complexity	Interval	Dimensionless
CPI	Cost/Budget Performance; Productivity	Ratio	Dimensionless
SPI	Schedule Performance	Ratio	Dimensionless
Cpk	Process Stability	Ratio	Dimensionless
DD	Module Stability	Ratio	Dimensionless
DRE	Quality Achieving Velocity	Ratio	Dimensionless

6. Appropriate Continuity

Valid indirect measures should not exhibit unexpected discontinuities i.e. they should be defined in all reasonable or expected situations. Thus, Measure A = Count1/Count2, may present problems if Count2 = 0 (when Measure A becomes infinity) or if Count1 = 0 (when Measure A becomes zero). Application of Appropriate continuity on the five indirect measures of the measurement model is as shown in table 27.

Table 27: Appropriate continuity

Indirect Measure (Derived Measure)	Equation	When Numerator is zero	When Denominator is zero
CPI	EV/AC	Earned Value (EV) can be zero if no activity is started against the WBS control accounts with respect to earning rules.	Every activity will consume a resource and a cost comes with every resource. Actual cost (AC) can be zero if there are no costs accounted.

SPI	EV/PV	Earned Value (EV) can be zero before the project starts when no activity is accomplished against the project tasks.	PV can be zero if the effort/cost and schedule is not estimated against the WBS Control Accounts.
Cpk	Yield to Conversion table i.e. C_{pk}	Cpk is based on DPMO which in turn is dependent on the defects captured against every opportunity.	
DD	Defects Open/FP	This is possible before the "Testing" starts and defects are not captured	This cannot be zero as every development will map to functionality/FPs.
DRE	Defects Resolved/ Total Defects	This is possible when the defects are captured but not resolved.	Every development will have some FPs. We have an empirically based formula to calculate the total defects from FPs.

7. Dimensional Consistency

A measure has dimensional consistency if the formulation of multiple measures into a composite measure is performed by a scientifically well-understood mathematical function. Basically this translates to the measures and their attributes agreeing as per dimensional analysis on both sides of the equation for the five indirect measures of the measurement model as shown in table 28.

Table 28: Dimensional Consistency

	Dimensional Consistency		
Measure	Attribute	Scale	Dimension Analysis
CPI	Cost/Budget Performance; Productivity	Ratio	Dimensionless.
SPI	Schedule Performance	Ratio	Dimensionless.
Cpk	Process Stability	Ratio	Dimensionless.
DD	Module Stability	Ratio	Dimensionless.
DRE	Quality Achieving Velocity	Ratio	Dimensionless.

4.2.2 Analysis of Kaner-Bond Questionnaire

While the seven theoretical validation criteria were at the measure level, Cem Kaner and Walter Bond proposed ten validation questions at the measurement model level [Kaner and Bond, 2004]. The objective is to prepare for the implementation of the measures in empirical/ practical situations.

1. What is the purpose of these eight measures?

All eight measures serve to track the status of a software project (through product, process and resource measures) for providing the right project status to the three groups of stakeholders i.e. initiators, implementers and beneficiaries.

2. What is the scope of these eight measures?

These eight measures should help to analyze projects with the program and modules/work streams within the project so as to make a reasonable comparison to make decisions for the project stakeholders. For instance, the program manager can use the measurement model to compare different projects in the program. Depending on the results, scarce resources can be allocated to the struggling area for improvement.

3. What attributes are we trying to measure?

The attributes of the measures are as shown below in table 29 and these are addressed as per the theoretical validation criteria proposed by Kitchenham et al.

Table 29: Attributes of the Measures

Measure	Attribute
LOC	Physical program size; size after development
FP	Functional program size; size before development
v(G)	Program Complexity
CPI	Cost/Budget Performance; Productivity

SPI	Schedule Performance
Cpk	Process Stability
DD	Module Stability
DRE	Quality Achieving Velocity

4. What is the natural scale of the attribute we are trying to measure?

The natural scale of the attribute is closely associated with the definition of the attribute. The scales of the eight measures are as shown in table 30.

Table 30: Natural Scales of the Measures

Measure/Attribute	Natural Scales
LOC/Size	Ratio Scale
FP/Size	Ratio Scale
v(G)/Complexity	Interval Scale
CPI/Cost	Ratio Scale
SPI/Schedule	Ratio Scale
Cpk/Quality	Ratio Scale
DD/Quality	Ratio Scale
DRE/Quality	Ratio Scale

5. What is the natural variability of the attribute?

Measurement is always performed under some degree of uncertainty resulting in some amount of variation in measurement:

- **Size Attribute**

  The variability for the size attributes is related to how LOC and FPs are measured. Variation in LOC is low as most of the development frameworks provide this count directly. But the variability in size when FPs is applied is medium because FP calculation is subjective and in the proposed measurement framework it is derived from tables derived empirically from historical data.

- **Complexity Attribute**

The variability for the complexity measure is low as v (G) is derived directly from development tools.

- **Cost and Schedule Attribute**

  The variability for the schedule and cost measures is medium as SPI and CPI calculations depend on the accuracy of the effort estimated and the work accomplished based on the granularity of earning rules.

- **Quality Attribute**

  The variability of quality attributes depends on how Cpk, DD and DRE are calculated. The variability of Cpk can be considered low as every opportunity is to identify a defect and this can be consistently tracked. However, variability of quality when using DD and DRE is medium as it is based on formulae and tables that are empirically validated. So the variation of the quality measures will be medium.

Therefore the natural variability in all the five attributes depends on how the respective measures are calculated and vary from low (for LOC, v (G) and Cpk) to medium (for FPs, SPI, CPI, DD and DRE).

6. What measuring instrument do we use to perform the measurement?

- LOC can be measured directly with standard development tools. There could even be a parser that strips comments and blank lines.
- FPs will come from a combination of Eclipse plug-in or an equivalent tool and the QSM table [QSM, 2009]. Eclipse is a software development environment comprising an integrated development environment (IDE) and an extensible plug-in system, to check the health of the code.
- Eclipse plug-in tool or an equivalent tool can give the count of v(G).
- Microsoft Project or an equivalent project management software package can provide SPI and CPI.

- The Cpk is basically the opportunity for a defect to occur. DPMO can be then converted to Cpk using "Yield to Sigma" conversion table.
- The DD and DRE can be calculated easily with a normal calculator.

7. What is the natural scale for the metrics?

The scale of the metric can be different from the scale of the underlying attribute. In all the eight measures, we are counting something and this suggests that the scale is either interval or ratio.

- The natural scale for v (G) is interval.
- The natural scale for all other measures is ratio. For example, a software component of DD 0.80 is twice as stable compared to a software component of DD 0.40. The same logic applies to LOC, FPs, SPI, CPI, Cpk and DRE.

8. What is the natural variability of reading from this instrument?

Variability might be seen in SPI and CPI as two people might estimate differently and hence different planned values (PV) for a same task. For all other measures, the variability will be low as the readings are coming from either the tables or development tools.

9. What is the relationship of the attribute to the metric value?

This is related to construct validity i.e. how do we know the metric measures that attribute. To address the threats on constructs validity, the measures and their objectives were given to software professionals for their feedback through a survey and then implemented in a real world project. This step is covered in detail in the empirical validation with a survey and case studies.

10. What are the natural and foreseeable side effects of using this instrument?

Any implementation of a measurement model is usually a change management initiative, which is not only related to technology, but also closely tied to cultural and people issues. If people's interests are dependent on the reported metrics, there is a tendency to hide facts or report incorrect data. This means all the eight measures will have some amount of side effects when applied in a software project until an atmosphere of frank and honest status reporting is created.

4.3 Analysis of Empirical Validation

According to the research methodology presented in chapter 3, a measure is considered empirically valid, if it confirms to the seven criteria namely:

1. Association
2. Attribute Validity
3. Discriminative Power
4. Instrument Validity
5. Predictability
6. Repeatability
7. Trackability

While each of the seven validation criteria are applicable for both case study and survey, for better management the validation criteria Discriminative Power, Instrument Validity and Trackability will be assessed in the case study, while the remaining four criteria i.e. association, attribute validity, predictability, and repeatability will be covered in the survey.

4.3.1 Analysis of the Case Study

4.3.1.1 Overview of the Case Study

A hybrid COTS software project which was a SAP Portal implementation in a core banking program was taken as the case study and appropriate thresholds, variances and control limits was set on the eight measures based on stakeholder needs and the CMMI level of the organization. The bank's strategy was to have a SAP

Portal for high frequency, customer facing transactions for the tellers, branch managers and back office personnel. The bank has close to 5,000 employees managing assets of over $25 billion and a customer base of about 700,000 people. According to Robert Stakes, crucial to case study research are not the methods of investigation, but the object of study [Stakes, 1999]. In this backdrop, the SAP Portal project was purposefully selected as the case study object for three main reasons:

- It was information-rich. The case study had to be investigated and implemented with a multitude of methods as the project was a part of the intellectual property (IP) development initiative from SAP AG Headquarters.
- It was a complex unit covering the entire suite of SAP banking application with aggressive time lines of delivery the project within six months and tight budgets.
- The project was contemporary with the architecture relying on Service oriented architecture (SOA) driven web services. Since SAP did not have a COTS Portal application for a bank, the project was a bespoke type of project with Java as the programming language accessing the SAP backend banking application with web services

The other key project details were:

- Budget: $2.1 million
- Duration: 1st February to 31st July, 2010.
- Project Implementation team size: 17 people.
- Industry: Bank/Financial Services (SEI CMMI Level 3)
- Product Scope: 17 Modules pertaining to SAP Banking Services (~ 300 FPs)
- Contracted days: 1,520 person-days (PDs).
- Key project stakeholders:
  - Initiators – Sponsor and Business Transformation lead
  - Implementers- Program Manager, Project Manager, Developer, Testers, and Business Analysts
  - Beneficiaries – Users i.e. Tellers.

4.3.1.2 Ensuring Reliability in the Case Study

As per the research design for reliability in the case study, the below three processes were adopted.

1. **Prolonged and Regular Data collection Processes.**

   Rational Unified Process (RUP) process was applied in this project so that quality data is collected. The RUP phases allowed the process to be presented in a 'waterfall'-styled project, although in essence the key to the process rested in the iterations of development that lie within all of the phases. Due to multiple iterations, the delivery was committed when stakeholders were satisfied for that iteration resulting in reliable data being collected and analyzed.

   One of the pre-requisites for the measurement program to be successful is to ensure that requirements are complete and non-volatile so that progress can be tracked against a fixed reference a.k.a performance measurement baseline (PMB). So stable requirements hold the key to the success of implementing the measurement model.

   This brings us to the selection of project implementation models. Generally, there are two implementation models applied in software projects: predictive lifecycle and adaptive software development. The predictive lifecycle favors optimization over adaptability, whereas adaptive software development is much more flexible while welcoming change. Incrementalism and iteration which are part of the adaptive (or agile) development help a project manage changes including implicit/unclear requirements along the way. Also according to Capers Jones adaptive software development works well for 1,000 FP range software projects [Jones, 2002].

At the same time a fundamental principle in software projects is changes introduced late in the project lifecycle costs far more than changes were introduced earlier in the cycle [Davis, Alan M, Bersoff, Edward and Comer, Edward, 1988]. So use of the predictive lifecycle (i.e. Waterfall) seeks to reduce the overall cost and risk by moving as much of the thinking up front as possible. Hence to get requirements completely (and be measured against the fixed target i.e. PMB) at an optimal cost and time, the best practices from both predictive lifecycle and adaptive software development methodologies were combined into a "hybrid methodology" commonly known as Rational Unified Pro (RUP) in this project/case study as shown in the figure 24 below.

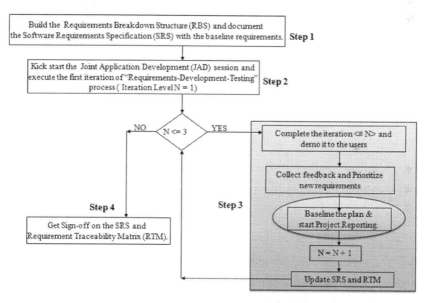

Figure 24: Four Step "Hybrid" RUP Methodology

Three iterations were decided based on the project organizational model. When the first iteration of the "Requirements-Development-Testing" activity was completed (box circled in figure 24), the project status reporting using the eight measures was started.

2. **Triangulation**

A variety of data sources were used in the project as opposed to relying solely upon one avenue of observation. Two types of triangulation techniques were employed.

  a. Data triangulation: Data was collected every week (time factor), on all the eight measures to cater to the needs of all stakeholders (people) in the project (space).
  b. Investigator/ Methodological triangulation: Once every four weeks, a different person in the project collected and analyzed the data and ultimately prepared the project status report using the eight measures.

3. **Member Checks**

The data on the eight measures was frequently shared every week with the stakeholders in the project for effective feedback. This enhanced the credibility and provided opportunities to correct errors in some instances. This also provided feedback thereby reducing the risk of project stakeholders reporting at a later date of any misunderstanding.

4.3.1.3 Data Collection

A. Product Measures

The first measure to capture was the **LOC**. This was a straight forward task as the SAP Netweaver developer studio used for the SAP Portal development provided this value directly.

To determine the **v (G)**, a freeware called "Eclipse plug-in" was used. This tool calculates the McCabe's cyclomatic complexity along with various other measures on the health of the code base. For example, the output from executing this tool for the "Transfers" function (one of the modules in the SAP Portal development) is as shown in the figure 25 below where the total McCabe's cyclomatic complexity for the module is the sum of the maximum McCabe's cyclomatic complexity for the individual packages such as TransfersComp.java, RecurringTransfersView.java et cetera.

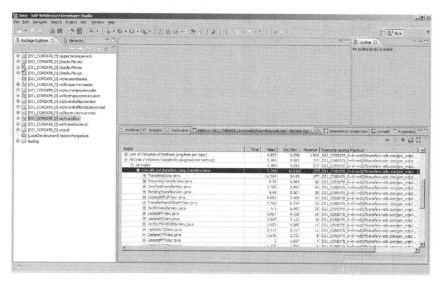

Figure 25: McCabe's Output from Eclipse plug-in

From the v (G) metric, the every method was categorized as low, medium and high complexity as per the tables provided by Frappier et al [Frappier et al, 1994] and endorsed by SEI. The complexity from every method was aggregated at the module level. From this complexity categorization and LOC count, the FP Languages table provided by QSM Inc [QSM, 2009] was leveraged to determine the number of **FPs** in the application.

For example, after the first iteration the v (G) for Transfers functionality (one of the 17 modules in scope) is 1,380 and the LOC is 18,603. As the cyclomatic complexity is more than 50, this functionality was categorized as highly complex. For a highly complex functionality with Java as the programming language, the FP languages table from QSM recommends 214 Lines of Code per FP [QSM, 2009].Hence the number of FPs in the Transfers component = 18,603/214 = 87. So using the Eclipse plug-in toll two metrics were determined i.e. v (G) (directly) and FP (indirectly).

B. Schedule and Cost Measures

After the product measures (LOC, FP and v (G)) were derived, the **SPI and CPI** measures were derived from EVM principles using Microsoft Project 2003 [Microsoft, 2011]. The three important steps used for calculating the SPI and CPI were:

1. **Building the Work Breakdown Structure (WBS)**

   Using the SRS document, a list of mutually exclusive elements were identified as the derivation of SPI and CPI for Earned Value (EV) analysis was to be done where the task i.e. work package (lowest element in the WBS) would be assigned to the developer. Each of the four main activities i.e. requirements, design, development and testing including deployment in the SDLC was a work package and the aggregation of the four respective work packages was the control account (CA).

2. **Assigning Planned Values (PV) to each terminal WBS element i.e. Control Account**

   After building the WBS, the planned value (PV) was assigned to each terminal element i.e. work package of the WBS by preparing software estimates such as high level effort (in person-days), project duration and resource cost. PV is the total cost of the work planned and is the product of Rate (cost of accomplishing the task by a resource) and Total Planned duration. With the base lined SRS (Step 1), the development was started with high level effort and the PV. Later when the project was re-baselined (first iteration of the "Requirements-Development-Testing"), the efforts were suitably changed in Microsoft Project for more accuracy.

3. **Establishing Earning Rules for each terminal WBS element**

   The values of SPI and CPI are dependent on the "earning rules" which quantify the work accomplished i.e. Earned Value (EV) for each terminal element of the WBS. The EV compares the actual work accomplished to the planned work up to a specific point in time. For this project the earning rules were defined as shown below in table 31 considering incremental and iterative development.

Table 31: Earning Rules for SPI and CPI

Deliverable	Percentage Applied for Earning Rules				
	25	50	75	90	100
RTM #	Technical design (TDD) is completed and development started	1st iteration of development completed and feeedback elicited from the stakeholders	2nd iteration of development completed and feeedback elicited from the stakeholders	3rd iteration of Development completed, testing is also completed and all defects are fixed	All 3 iterations are completed. Buffer consumed. SRS and TDD completed and signed-off

C. Quality Measures

The results pertaining to the three measures on quality are explained below.

1. To calculate the **Cpk** every test case was considered as an opportunity for a defect to potentially surface. For example 105 out of 117 test cases executed failed in the Transfers functionality at the first iteration. This translated to 897,436 defects for 1 million opportunities (DPMO) providing a sigma level of 0.2.

2. **DD** was used to compare the number of defects against the number of FPs in each software component. In the Transfers functionality (one of the 17 modules in the project), 105 defects were identified for 87 FPs giving a DD of $105/87 = 1.21$.

3. **DRE** is the ratio of the defects removed at a specific phase to the total possible defects. It provides information on the rate at which defects are resolved. As explained in chapter 3, to find the potential count of the total defects in a new software project, Capers Jones proposes to use FPs to the power 1.25 [Jones, 2002]. For example, the total number of defects that can potentially exist in the Transfers functionality was FPs to the power 1.25 i.e. 87 to the power 1.25 which is 265. After the

first iteration was completed, 12 defects were fixed giving a DRE of 12/265 = 0.05.

The complete measurement framework implemented in the case study is as shown in figure.26 below.

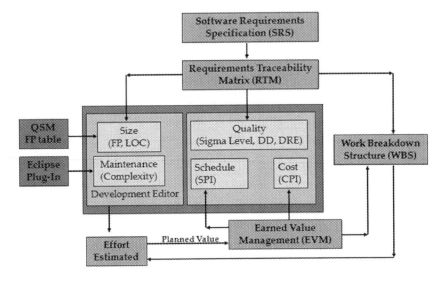

Figure 26: Measurement Model in the Case Study

4.3.1.4 Case Study 2: Uncontrolled Instance

To demonstrate a cause and effect hypothesis, the case study should also indicate that a phenomenon occurs after a certain treatment is given to a subject (controlled setting), and that the phenomenon does not occur in the absence of the treatment (uncontrolled setting).

While the eight measures that were applied were in the SAP Portal project, another similar project – an online banking application project (refer table 32 below for similarities) was studied in the same program at the same time. However, the eight measures were not applied and instead the project tracking was done with earned value management (EVM) (using just the SPI and CPI measures) which is one of the most popular techniques for tracking project performance today.

On 15th May 2010, the SPI for this project was at 0.96 with the planned completion date of 30th July 2010. On 9th July, the SPI was at 0.99 still showing the same planned completion date of 30th July. But on 30th July, when the project was expected to be completed (and transitioned to the maintenance team), there were many defects that were still open making the project incomplete. After further review of the incomplete deliverables, the project completion date was then moved to 20th November ultimately resulting in a delayed and unsuccessful project.

Table 32: Similarities between Two Case Studies

SL #	Project Characteristics	SAP Portal Application	Internet Banking Application
1	Statement of Work(SOW)	Implementation of the teller Application for the bank's front end staff for frequently used transactions	Implementation of the Internet banking application for the bank's end customers.
2	Team Size	17	19
3	Function Points (Size)	282	300 (approximately)
4	Duration	1st February to 31st July 2010	10th January to 31st July 2010
5	Development Platform/ Project Class	Java and SAP (4GL)	Java and SAP(4GL)
6	SEI CMMI (Quality Level)	Level 3	Level 3
7	Budget	2.1 million CAD	2.4 million CAD
8	Contracted Effort	1520 person days	1660 person days
8	Project Type	Bespoke	Bespoke
9	Stakeholders	Tellers/Users, project team, Business Transformation lead and program Manager	Users, project team, Business Transformation lead and program Manager

Two prominent issues come up with the usage of the SPI as a project performance metrics in this case study.

1. Traditionally, EVM tracks schedule variances not in units of time, but in units of currency (e.g. dollars) or sometimes quantity (e.g. person days) considering that it is more natural to speak of schedule performance in units of time. SPI or more specifically schedule variance (SV) says project is $500 000 late. But it doesn't provide information on how many months or days is the delay. In addition, an unfavorable schedule variance does not necessarily imply that project is behind schedule as by itself, the SPI reveals no critical path information.

2. As mentioned before, SPI is the ratio between EV and PV. At the end of the project, if the project has delivered everything that was planned, EV and PV must be equal making SPI equal to 1. This characteristic without accounting for the deadline, questions the usefulness and predictability of SPI because after the planned end of the project, PV remains constant while the EV will continue to grow until the actual end of the project. For example, if the project is planned to be finished in 10 months, and if the EV after 10 months is 70%, it is 30 % behind schedule. Finally at the end of the project (as eventually the project has to be completed) the EV will be equal to your PV when all the deliverables are completed. This according to EVM means that the project is completed "on time" even though it is couple of months late. Even worse is if the project "continues" after the planned end date and for some reason if nothing is done say for three months, the SPI will be the same for three months as it still refers to the baselined PV/duration. In addition, a project can languish near completion (e.g. SPI = 0.95) and never be flagged as outside acceptable numerical tolerance. This is exactly what has happened in this case study where SPI was used to track the project performance.

Certain researchers maintain that SPI is good and reliable in first two thirds of the project and it starts to be defective over the final third of a project's lifecycle [Lipke, 2003; Vandevoorde, S. and Vanhoucke M, 2006]. According to Fleming, The SPI should be used in conjunction with other schedule information [Fleming, 1992]. In addition, while the SPI measure initially indicated that the project was on schedule, it did not portray the true project status as the quality (or product) measures particularly on defect prevention and removal were never reported and hence no corrective action was taken. If the weekly status reports had the quality measures in them (which was deteriorating every week), perhaps the project stakeholders would have been better prepared to take suitable corrective actions.

4.3.2 Analysis of Survey Results

4.3.2.1 Overview of the Survey

The unit of analysis in the survey was project stakeholders, such as sponsor, project manager, developer, tester and user to name a few who have worked in hybrid and bespoke software projects. The sampling frame included:

- Professionals from software companies such as IBM, Accenture, SAP, HP et cetera
- Professionals registered in the LinkedIn groups such as IT Program and Project Managers, Measurement and Analysis Forum, Software Testing & Quality Assurance, Software Engineering Productivity, and Software User Assistance
- IT stakeholders in multi-national non-IT conglomerates such as GE, Siemens, P&G, Shell, et cetera.
- Professionals in software engineering conferences such as IEEE, ASQ, SQDG, PMI et cetera.

In addition quotas were set to ensure that a sufficient number of respondents from the sampling frame represented all three types of stakeholders.

4.3.2.2 Data Collection in the Survey: Descriptive Statistics

As the survey responses were ordinal data, the measures such as mean, standard deviation and variance were not used in the descriptive statistics As mentioned in the research approach chapter, descriptive statistics included five statistical techniques.

1. Stakeholder Profile
2. Bar charts and Scatter plots
3. Skewness and Kurtosis
4. Central tendency summarized by median (with box plots) and mode.
5. Variability summarized by range and inter-quartile range

1. Stakeholder Profile

The survey responses were from 123 professionals who shared 1899 years of software project experience. These respondents were from 31 countries from Vietnam in the far-east to Chile in the far-west and included Chief Information officers (CIO), Directors, Program Managers, Project Managers, Business Analysts, Quality Managers, Developers, testers, Architects, Metrics specialists, and Users. The organizations of these respondents were at different CMMI levels and were from industry sectors such as Professional services, Telecom, Banking, Insurance, Health care, Pharmaceuticals, Energy and Retail. The profile details of the survey respondents are as shown in the figure 27 below.

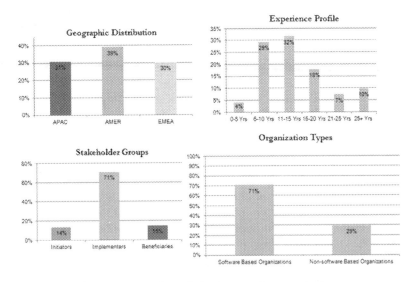

Figure 27: Profile of the Survey Respondents

2. Bar charts

Below table 33 gives the number of responses for each of the nine measures

Table 33: Frequency of Survey Responses

#	Measure	Strongly Disagree	Disagree	Neither Agree or disagree	Agree	Strongly Agree	Total Responses
1	FP	3	6	19	77	10	115
2	LOC	9	23	43	37	7	119
3	V(G)	3	6	17	42	7	75
4	CPI	1	4	15	72	17	109
5	SPI	2	8	21	61	20	111
6	Cpk	2	7	25	48	14	96
7	DD	1	9	20	58	24	102
8	DRE	2	5	18	55	22	102
9	Om	1	10	21	78	9	119

Based on the above table, the bar charts for each of the measures is as shown below

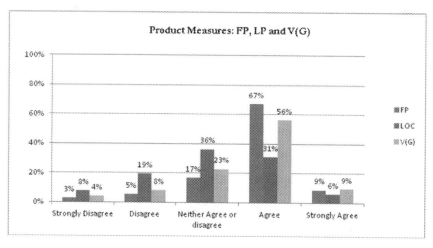

Figure 28: Product Measures i.e. FP, LOC and V(G)

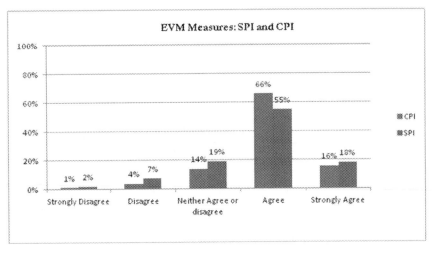

Figure 29: EVM Measures i.e. SPI and CPI

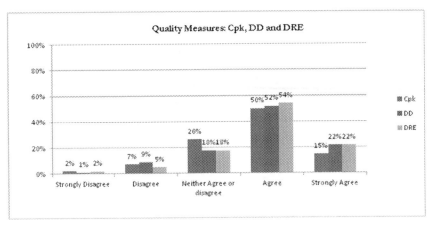

Figure 30: Quality Measures i.e. Cpk, DD and DRE

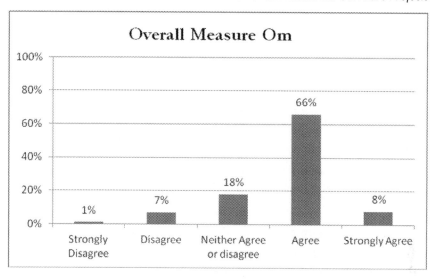

Figure 31: Response for the Overall Measure i.e. Om

3. Skewness and Kurtosis

As mentioned in chapter 3, skewness is a measure of the asymmetry of the probability distribution and the skewness value can be positive or negative, or even undefined. The skewness values for the nine measures including the overall measure OM is as shown in the table 34 below.

Table 34: Skewness Values of Survey Responses

	FP	LOC	VG	CPI	SPI	Cpk	DD	DRE	Om
Skewness	-1.4	-0.3	-1.0	-1.0	-0.9	-0.7	-0.7	-1.0	-0.9

The table above shows that the skew is negative for all the nine measures. A negative skew indicates that the tail on the left side of the probability density function is longer than the right side and the bulk of the values (possibly including the median) lie to the right of the mean.

123

Again as mentioned in Chapter 3, kurtosis is the measure of the "peakedness" of the probability distribution. The kurtosis values for the nine measures including the overall measure Om is as shown in the table 35 below.

Table 35: Kurtosis Values of Survey Responses

	FP	LOC	VG	CPI	SPI	Cpk	DD	DRE	Om
Kurtosis	2.8	-0.4	1.1	2.7	0.9	0.6	0.4	1.4	0.8

The table above shows that the kurtosis values are **Platykurtic** (negative) and **Leptokurtic** (positive). When compared to a normal distribution, a platykurtic data set (only for LOC) has a flatter peak around its mean, which causes thin tails within the distribution. The flatness or the increased spread results from the data being less concentrated around its mean, due to large variations within observations. Leptokurtic distributions (for the remaining eight measures) have higher peaks around the mean compared to normal distributions, which leads to thick tails on both sides. These peaks result from the data being highly concentrated around the mean, lower spread, and lower variations within observations.

4. Central tendency summarized by median for the nine measures.

As said before, the Central tendency will be represented using the median which is the middle value in a data set that has been arranged in numerical order so that exactly half the data is above the median and half is below it. The Central tendency is represented using five measures as shown below in table 36.

Table 36: Central tendency summarized by Median

	FP	LOC	VG	CPI	SPI	Cpk	DD	DRE	Om
Minimum Value	1.0	1.0	1.0	1.0	1.0	1.0	1.0	1.0	1.0
1st Quartile (Q1)	4.0	2.0	3.0	4.0	3.0	3.0	3.0	4.0	3.0

Median (Q2)	4.0	3.0	4.0	4.0	4.0	4.0	4.0	4.0	4.0
3rd Quartile (Q3)	4.0	4.0	4.0	4.0	4.0	4.0	4.0	4.0	4.0
Maximum Value	5.0	5.0	5.0	5.0	5.0	5.0	5.0	5.0	5.0

5. Variability summarized by range and inter-quartile range (Q3-Q1)

Table 37: Variability summarized by Range and IQR

	FP	LOC	VG	CPI	SPI	Cpk	DD	DRE	Om
Range	4.00	4.00	4.00	4.00	4.00	4.00	4.00	4.00	3.00
Inter-Quartile Range (IQR)	0.00	2.00	1.00	0.00	1.00	1.00	1.00	0.00	1.00

4.3.2.3 Analysis of Survey: Inferential Statistics

As mentioned in the research design chapter, the inferential statistics has four statistical techniques. They are:

1. Net Promoter Score (NPS)
2. Pearson's Correlation
3. Regression Analysis
4. Other Hypothesis Testing
   a. Similar Measures (HM)
   b. Stakeholder groups (HS)

1. NPS Analysis

In NPS analysis, respondents who rated 1 (strongly disagree) or 2 (disagree) on the measures were categorized as critics. Those who responded with 3 (neither agree nor disagree) were grouped as neutral, while promoters were the ones who rated 4 (agree) or 5 (strongly agree) on the measures. In the survey, 74% of the 110 respondents "promote" that these eight measures can serve as a core set for an objective status of a software project. The complete promoter, neutral and critics scores for the nine measures are as shown in figure 32 below.

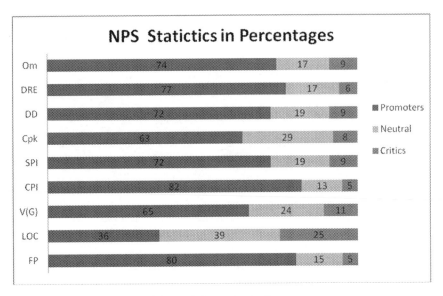

Figure 32: NPS Statistics in Percentages

As mentioned in the chapter on literature review, the stakeholders have different value propositions. Hence in formulating the goal in chapter 3 the primary concerns of initiators were taken as schedule and cost, implementers' concerns were considered as size while quality was taken as the main issue users would have in the software project. Using the responses collected in the survey, this section validates the "value proposition" hypothesis in literature study to see if this is true and at the same time throws more light on the eight measures.

Table 38 below shows the NPS efficiency (which is % of Promoters - % of Critics) on the nine measures based on the responses of the three groups of stakeholders.

Table 38: NPS efficiency based on stakeholder groups

#	Measure	NPS Efficiency of beneficiaries	NPS Efficiency of implementers	NPS Efficiency of initiators
1	FP	69%	67%	75%
2	LOC	33%	8%	12%
3	V(G)	100%	45%	60%
4	CPI	88%	76%	71%
5	SPI	94%	58%	62%
6	Cpk	86%	54%	54%
7	DD	79%	60%	69%
8	DRE	79%	67%	67%

The results are very much in line with the value propositions derived in step 1 of the GQM Model where the initiators were concerned with schedule and cost, implementers were concerned with size, and beneficiaries were looking for quality.

2. Pearson's Correlation test

The survey data was further analyzed with pearson's correlation analysis to understand how the dependent and the independent variables are associated. There was a fair degree of correlation between the overall measure and each of the eight measures (except for FP) which is shown below. This satisfies the **association** validity criteria for empirical validation which states that – a metric has association validity if it has a direct, linear statistical correlation with an external quality factor which in this case is the Overall Measure (Om). Figure 33 shows the Pearson's correlation co-efficient between each of the measures and Om (except for LOC).

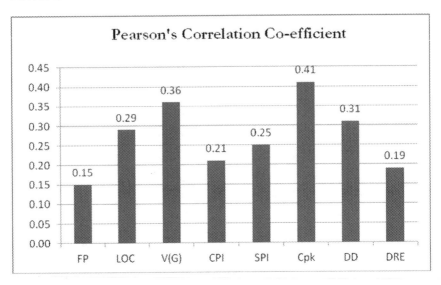

Figure 33: Correlation between the Means of 8 Measures and Om

Hence this thesis, compute t using the following formula:

$$t = \frac{r\sqrt{N-2}}{\sqrt{1-r^2}}$$

The t-values are as shown in the table 39 below.

Table 39: t-values

Measure	Sample Sizes	DF	r-value	t-value
FP	114	112	0.15	1.62
LOC	117	115	0.29	3.40
V(G)	93	91	0.36	3.95
CPI	108	106	0.21	2.26
SPI	111	109	0.25	2.78
Cpk	96	94	0.41	4.78
DD	112	110	0.31	3.60
DRE	102	100	0.19	1.97

The p values for the above values of t and N-2 DF for the 95% confidence interval is as shown below in table 40.

Table 40: p-values

Measure	DF	P-value from 2-tailed test	Inference
FP	112	0.11	Accept Ho.
LOC	115	0.00	Reject Ho
V(G)	91	0.00	Reject Ho
CPI	106	0.03	Reject Ho
SPI	109	0.01	Reject Ho
Cpk	94	0.00	Reject Ho
DD	110	0.00	Reject Ho
DRE	100	0.05	Reject Ho

The analysis shows that there is no association between FP and Om. However there is a correlation/association between remaining seven measures and the overall measure Om.

3. Regression Analysis

The goal of regression analysis is to determine the values of parameters for a function that cause the function to best fit a set of data observations that are provided. The regression summary is as shown in the table 41 below.

Table 41: Regression summary

Regression Statistics									
Multiple R	0.6729								
R Square	0.4528								
Adjusted R Square	0.3486								
Standard Error	0.6671								
Observations	51.0000								

ANOVA								
	df	SS	MS	F	Significance F			
Regression	8.0000	15.4661	1.9333	4.3443	0.0007			
Residual	42.0000	18.6907	0.4450					
Total	50.0000	34.1569						
	Coefficient	Standard Error	t Stat	P-value	Lower 95%	Upper 95%	Lower 95.0%	Upper 95.0%
Intercept	0.4771	0.6835	0.6981	0.4890	-0.9022	1.8564	-0.9022	1.8564
FP	-0.2031	0.1389	-1.4618	0.1512	-0.4835	0.0773	-0.4835	0.0773
LOC	0.0915	0.1088	0.8408	0.4052	-0.1281	0.3112	-0.1281	0.3112
V(G)	-0.1241	0.1341	-0.9251	0.3602	-0.3947	0.1466	-0.3947	0.1466
CPI	0.3169	0.1875	1.6900	0.0984	-0.0615	0.6952	-0.0615	0.6952
SPI	-0.0187	0.1537	-0.1217	0.9037	-0.3288	0.2914	-0.3288	0.2914
Cpk	0.4535	0.1404	3.2294	0.0024	0.1701	0.7368	0.1701	0.7368
DD	0.0647	0.1525	0.4244	0.6734	-0.2430	0.3725	-0.2430	0.3725
DRE	0.2577	0.1636	1.5750	0.1228	-0.0725	0.5879	-0.0725	0.5879

The Regression model derived is:

Om (Y) = 0.4771 - 0.2031*FP + 0.0915*LOC -0.1241*V (G) + 0.3169*CPI -0.0187*SPI +0.4535*Cpk + 0.0647*DD + 0.2577*DRE

This model has 45.3% of the variability (Value of R-square is 0.4528) in the dependent variable (i.e. Om) explained in the regression model. According to Schneidewind if the value of R^2 i.e. goodness of fit is greater than 0.5 the regression model provides a good amount of predictably [Schneidewind, 1991]. Here the value of the goodness of fit is close to 0.50 and hence the model coming out of Multiple Linear Regression will be adopted. Hence this model illustrates a good amount of **Predictability** thereby satisfying the second criterion for empirical validation pertaining to the survey.

The hypothesis testing will be to test if each of the eight measures is related to the overall measure Om. Specifically the null and alternate hypothesis for each of the eight co-efficient will be:

Ho: $\beta k = 0$
Ha: $\beta k \neq 0$

where k is from 1 to 8 for the eight measures and β is the respective co-efficient of the eight measures. The results are as shown in the table 42 below.

Table 42: Regression Analysis Hypothesis

	Coefficient	Standard Error	Mod (t-statistic)	P-Value	Inference
Intercept	0.477	0.683	0.698	0.488	Accept Ho
FP	-0.203	0.139	1.462	0.150	Accept Ho
LOC	0.092	0.109	0.841	0.404	Accept Ho
V(G)	-0.124	0.134	0.925	0.359	Accept Ho
CPI	0.317	0.187	1.690	0.097	Accept Ho
SPI	-0.019	0.154	0.122	0.904	Accept Ho
Cpk	0.453	0.140	3.229	0.002	Reject Ho
DD	0.065	0.152	0.424	0.673	Accept Ho
DRE	0.258	0.164	1.575	0.121	Accept Ho

The above table concludes that sample evidence supports the proposition that the overall measure Om is related to the seven measures except to the Sigma level Cpk. This means seven of the eight measures except Cpk has a bearing on the regression model.

4. Other Hypothesis Testing

D1. Relationship between Similar Constructs/Measures (HM)

As mentioned in Chapter 3, the hypothesis testing is conducted with Chi-square testing where the null hypothesis H_0 assumes that there is no association between the variables (in other words, one variable does not vary according to the other variable), while the alternative hypothesis H$_a$ claims that some association does exist.

- LOC and FP. The null hypothesis (HM-Ho1) is that there is no association between the LOC and FP measures.
- SPI and CPI. The null hypothesis (HM-Ho2) is that there is no association between the SPI and CPI measures.
- Cpk and DD. The null hypothesis (HM-Ho3) is that there is no association between the Cpk and DD measures.
- DRE and DD. The null hypothesis (HM-Ho4) is that there is no association between the DRE and DD measures.
- DRE and Cpk. The null hypothesis (HM-Ho5) is that there is no association between the DRE and Cpk measures.

The null hypothesis in all the above five cases will be rejected if the p-value will be less than α value of 0.05. The data sets included each of the eight measures and the overall measure (Om). The p-values and the inference are as shown in the table 43 below.

Table 43: Relationship between Similar Constructs

Sl #	Test	p-value	Inference
1	LOC v/s FP	0.485	The p-value is greater than the value of 0.05. Hence null hypothesis is accepted i.e. the respondents saw LOC and FP measures independently.
2	SPI v/s CPI	0.0046	The p-value is less than the value of 0.05. Hence null hypothesis is rejected i.e. the respondents saw association between SPI and CPI measures.
3	Cpk v/s DD	0.0038	The p-value is less than the value of 0.05. Hence null hypothesis is rejected i.e. the respondents saw association between Cpk and DD measures.
4	DD v/s DRE	0.018	The p-value is less than the value of 0.05. Hence null hypothesis is rejected i.e. there is association between DRE and DD
5	DRE v/s Cpk	0.041	The p-value is less than the value of 0.05. Hence null hypothesis is rejected i.e. there is association between DRE and Cpk

D2. Relationship between the three stakeholders groups (HS)

As mentioned in Chapter 3, the Kruskal-Wallis (KW) test assumes that the variables under consideration have underlying continuous distributions. The KW test was applied on the three stakeholder groups (initiators, implementers and beneficiaries) on the nine measures.

The null hypothesis HS-Ho1 to HS-Ho9 state that the k samples for each of the nine measures come from the same population. This means if the null hypothesis is true, then the test statistic, H, used in the KW procedure is greater than the critical value. In this case there will be nine values of H for the nine measures. If the critical value for $a = .05$ with $df = k-1 = 3-1 = 2$ is X. If the Hi > X, we reject the null hypothesis concluding that the samples come from the different population. Following are the nine definitions of null hypothesis.

1. HS-Ho1 states that the 3 sample data coming from initiators, implementers and beneficiaries for FP measure comes from the same population.
2. HS-Ho2 states that the 3 sample data coming from initiators, implementers and beneficiaries for LOC measure comes from the same population.
3. HS-Ho3 states that the 3 sample data coming from initiators, implementers and beneficiaries for V(G) measure comes from the same population.
4. HS-Ho4 states that the 3 sample data coming from initiators, implementers and beneficiaries for CPI measure comes from the same population.
5. HS-Ho5 states that the 3 sample data coming from initiators, implementers and beneficiaries for SPI measure comes from the same population.
6. HS-Ho6 states that the 3 sample data coming from initiators, implementers and beneficiaries for Cpk measure comes from the same population.
7. HS-Ho7 states that the 3 sample data coming from initiators, implementers and beneficiaries for DD measure comes from the same population.

8. HS-Ho8 states that the 3 sample data coming from initiators, implementers and beneficiaries for DRE measure comes from the same population.

9. HS-Ho9 states that the 3 sample data coming from initiators, implementers and beneficiaries for Om measure comes from the same population.

The null hypothesis in all the above five cases will be rejected if the p-value will be less than α value of 0.05. The p-values are as shown in the table 44 below.

Table 44: p-values and hypothesis inference

#	Measures	p-value	Inference
1	FP	0.123	The p-value is greater than the value of 0.05. Hence null hypothesis is accepted i.e. the initiators, implementers and beneficiaries see no difference in the FP measure.
2	LOC	0.027	The p-value is less than the value of 0.05. Hence null hypothesis is rejected i.e. the initiators, implementers and beneficiaries see the LOC measure differently.
3	V(G)	0.241	The p-value is greater than the value of 0.05. Hence null hypothesis is accepted i.e. the initiators, implementers and beneficiaries see no difference in the V(G) measure.
4	CPI	0.641	The p-value is greater than the value of 0.05. Hence null hypothesis is accepted i.e. the initiators, implementers and beneficiaries see no difference in the CPI measure.
5	SPI	0.211	The p-value is greater than the value of 0.05. Hence null hypothesis is accepted i.e. the initiators, implementers and beneficiaries see no difference in the SPI measure.
6	Cpk	0.131	The p-value is greater than the value of 0.05. Hence null hypothesis is accepted i.e. the initiators, implementers and beneficiaries see no difference in the Cpk measure.
7	DD	0.149	The p-value is greater than the value of 0.05. Hence null hypothesis is accepted i.e. the initiators, implementers and beneficiaries see no difference in the DD measure.

8	DRE	0.295	The p-value is greater than the value of 0.05. Hence null hypothesis is accepted i.e. the initiators, implementers and beneficiaries see no difference in the DRE measure.
9	Om	0.376	The p-value is greater than the value of 0.05. Hence null hypothesis is accepted i.e. the initiators, implementers and beneficiaries see no difference in the Om measure

4.3.3.4 Ensuring Reliability in the Survey

In this research thesis, the reliability tests on the survey are conducted at two levels.

1. Reliability of the survey questionnaire

   The two reliability tests that are applied on the survey questionnaire are:

   a. Test-Retest Reliability Test
   b. Cronbach's Internal Consistency test

2. Reliability of the survey response data

1. Reliability of the survey questionnaire

Before the survey was deployed to address the reliability and validity threats of the survey questionnaire, three pilot studies were conducted on a small group of stakeholders from different companies and countries. The first pilot study was to ensure that the survey questions address the content, criterion, and construct validity objectives. Feedback was collected and the survey questions were deliberated; however no responses were recorded. To ensure there was no ambiguity these questions were reworked. Then the second pilot study was conducted on the same group and their responses were recorded when there was no feedback on the way the questions were constructed. To reduce the "carry over" effect between the two testings, after six weeks, the same questionnaire was again sent to the same group for their responses after six weeks as part of the third pilot study. This was taken as their final response for survey analysis. The Pearson's correlation for all the measures between the second pilot test and the final survey response i.e. the third study was close to the recommended threshold value of 0.90 between the data sets of the two tests as shown in the figure 33 below satisfying the **repeatability criteria** for empirical validation [Schneidewind,1992].

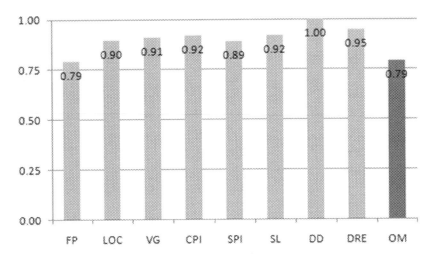

Figure 34: Correlation Values for Survey Validity

As a second test for reliability, the Cronbach's alpha for the same data set was carried out. The Cronbach's alpha is a measure of internal consistency i.e. how closely related a set of items are as a group. It is basically an average inter-correlation among the items. The overall value of Cronbach's alpha was found to be 0.78 which again exceeded the threshold of 0.70 set for **repeatability criteria** for reliability/ repeatability [Schneidewind, 1992].

2. Reliability of the survey response data

For the measurement error to be small, best possible reliable data should be available. Reliability of the data in the eight measures is compared using the index of variation (IV) and is an indication of how much an observed score can be expected to be the same if observed again. IV is simply a ratio of the standard deviation to the mean. Smaller the IV, more reliable is the measurements. Table 45 below indicates that summary response data for FP and CPI is more reliable than the data collected for LOC.

Table 45: Index of Variation

	FP	LOC	VG	CPI	SPI	SL	DD	DRE	Overall
Reliability (Index of Variation)	0.19	0.30	0.23	0.19	0.23	0.22	0.22	0.21	0.20

4.3.3.5 Debate on having LOC in the Measurement Model

While the survey responses were not positive for LOC, the debate on the application of LOC to software measurements has persisted for a long time. There are many research papers that debate the value of LOC in software engineering. According to Capers Jones, "the use of LOC metric for productivity and quality studies is to be regarded as professional malpractice" [Jones, 2008]. Even in the survey, there were extreme cases where some respondents strongly agreed that LOC measures the size of the software project objectively after development and should be part of the core set of measures, while there were many more who felt otherwise. To gain better understanding, further analysis was exclusively carried out on the LOC relevant survey data.

The first analysis in table 46 was the LOC scores given by respondents of software based organizations and non-software based organization. The analysis shows no discrimination between the types of the organization in relation to this measure.

Table 46: Analysis of LOC data based on Organization types

	Non Software Organizations	Software Organization
Median LOC Score	4.00	4.00
Reliability (Index of Variation)	0.34	0.32
Promoters %	32%	37%

Chi-Square Test	P-value is 0.65. As P-value is > 0.05, null hypothesis is accepted implying that the data set is the "same".
Conclusion	This indicates that there is no difference in the way respondents from non-software organizations and software organizations look at LOC.

The second analysis in table 47 was the LOC scores given by software project implementers and others (i.e. initiators and beneficiaries). The analysis is as shown in the table 47 indicated little differences regardless of the role of respondents in the software project.

Table 47: Analysis of LOC data based on Stakeholder types

	Implementers	Others
Median LOC Score	3.00	3.50
Promoters %	32%	55%
Reliability (Index of Variation)	0.35	0.25
Chi-Square Test	P-value is 0.57. As P-value is > 0.05, null hypothesis is accepted implying that the data set is the "same".	
Conclusion	Though the first three measures show some distinction, the Chi-square test indicates that there is no difference in the way implementers and initiators/beneficiaries look at LOC.	

The third analysis in table 48 was the LOC scores between developers and non-developers. This was done to see if the developers who write the code can provide any more specific information. The analysis is as shown in the below table shows little distinction between the LOC value as seen by developers and non-developers.

Table 48: Analysis of LOC data based on Developer Skills

	Developers	Non-Developers
Median LOC Score	3.00	3.00
Reliability (Index of Variation)	0.29	0.33
Promoters %	28%	37%
Chi-Square Test	P-value is 0.84. As P-value is > 0.05, null hypothesis is accepted implying that the data set is the "same".	

Conclusion	All these measures indicate that there is no difference in the way developers and non-developers look at LOC.

The fourth analysis in table 49 was between the LOC scores and McCabe's cyclomatic complexity i.e. v (G). As LOC and v (G) are dependent on the programmer's skills, this analysis was done to see if the survey data can throw any interesting information. The analysis is as shown in the table below.

Table 49: Analysis of LOC and v (G)

	LOC	McCabe's complexity
Median Score	3.00	3.50
Reliability (Index of Variation)	0.34	0.30
Promoters %	36%	65%
Pearson's Correlation	The Pearson's r for LOC and v (G) data was found to 0.18 which indicates poor correlation between the two measures. As LOC and McCabe's cyclomatic complexity are related, the correlation should have been higher than 0.5.	
Chi-Square Test	P-value is 0.80. As P-value is > 0.05, null hypothesis is accepted implying that the data set is the "same" i.e. there is no difference in the way respondents looked at LOC and v (G).	
Conclusion	If there was no correlation between the LOC and v (G) data sets, they should have come from different data sets. But as the P-value from the Chi-square test is greater than 0.05, it shows that there is no difference in the data sets. This "anomaly" could be because: 1. LOC is more often used than McCabe's cyclomatic complexity in software projects [Fenton, 2006]. Hence respondents have seen the challenges or failure of using LOC in projects. 2. LOC is simpler to understand than McCabe's cyclomatic complexity for the respondents to give opinion. In addition, due to the technical nature, developers and architects are generally more educated in LOC and v (G) than sponsors and users.	

Even with all its problems/deficiencies, LOC is amongst the three measures (along with McCabe's cyclomatic complexity and Function points) that are extensively and routinely used in the industry [Fenton, 2006]. Steve McConnell states "For most organizations, despite its problems, the LOC measure is the workhorse technique for measuring size of past projects and for creating early-in-the-project estimates of new projects. The LOC measure is the *lingua franca* of software estimation, and it is normally a good place to start, as long as you keep its limitations in mind" [McConnell, 2006, pp 199]. Hence LOC is included in the measurement model with the rider that it should not be the only measure used to make decisions pertaining to product size in the project and should be used along with Function Points.

4.3.3.6 Other Feedback in the Survey

Some respondents in the survey wanted to have risk and requirements volatility measures in the measurement framework. Risks is a product of two components - Probability of the event happening and Impact/loss the event can cause. The 'utility' type measure of risk is quite useful for prioritizing risks (the bigger the number the 'greater' the risk) but it is generally meaningless as one cannot get both the probability and the impact numbers in the project. In addition risk exists in a given context; if there is a challenge in meeting schedule or cost or quality objectives. Each of these three attributes are already captured in the measurement framework as SPI, CPI and Cpk/DD/DRE measures respectively. Hence risk as a measure was not included in the measurement model.

Requirements volatility is a measure of how much requirements change after a critical point in the SDLC. It is the ratio of total number of requirements change (add, delete and modify) to total number of requirements for a given period of time. The reason for the change could range from lapse in developer understanding to changes in customer needs as a result of shift in market conditions. This growth/creep/evolution ultimately results in volatility ultimately impacting the schedule, cost and quality in the project. However each of these three attributes i.e. schedule, cost and quality is already captured in the measurement model as SPI, CPI and Cpk/DD/DRE measures respectively. Hence requirements volatility as a measure was not included in the measurement model.

4.4 Conclusion

The research analysis here covered both theoretical validation and empirical validation of the eight measures of the measurement model. Theoretical validation included assessing the measurement model against the seven validation criteria. It was further bolstered with the application of ten questions of Kaner and Bond. The empirical validation which forms the bulk of the analysis included case studies on two real world implementation projects and a survey from 123 industry practitioners. Based on the analysis, the next chapter will exclusively deal with the research results.

Chapter 5

Discussion on Research Results

5.1 Introduction

This chapter discusses the results found in relation to the two research questions and existing body of knowledge (Bok). This chapter demonstrates the interpretation of the findings and outlining what they mean. This chapter is organized into three main sections:

- Discuss the research results from theoretical validation.
- Discuss the research results from empirical validation - the case study and the survey.
- Discuss the impact of this research to the existing software metrics body of knowledge (BoK).

5.2 Results of Theoretical Validation

The seven theoretical validation criteria are summarized below in table 50.

Table 50: Summarized Theoretical Validation Criteria

SI	Criteria/Attribute	Definition	LOC	FP	V(G)	CPI	SPI	Cpk	DD	DRE
	Measure Type		Direct	Direct	Direct	Indirect (EV/AC)	Indirect (EV/PV)	Indirect	Indirect (Defects Open/FP)	Indirect (Defects Resolved/Total Defects)
	Definition		Physical program size	Functional program size	Decision path based Program Complexity	Variation/Adherence to Budget	Variation/Adherence to Schedule	SDLC Process Stability	Module Program Code Stability	Quality Achieving Velocity
1	Scale Validity	A measure has scale validity if it is defined on an explicit, appropriate scale such that all meaningful transformations of the measure are admissible. Each scale type (nominal, ordinal, interval and ratio) denotes a specific set of transformations that dictate how the measure can be used.	Ratio Scale	Ratio Scale	Interval Scale	Ratio Scale	Ratio Scale	Ratio Scale	Ratio Scale	Ratio Scale
2	Appropriate Granularity	A measure has appropriate granularity if the mapping from attribute to measure is not too finely or coarsely grained. The right granularity should reflect the goals of the measurement.	Fine	Medium	Fine	Fine	Fine	Fine	Fine	Fine
3	Representation Condition	A measure basically maps real world attributes to a numerical domain i.e. to a set of integers, rational numbers, or real numbers. This mapping is called representation or homomorphism, because the measure represents the attribute in the numerical world.	Yes	Yes	Yes	Yes	Yes	Yes	Yes	Yes
4	Unit Validity	A measure has unit validity if the measures used are an appropriate means of measuring the attribute.	Standard Definition	Standard Definition	Standard Definition	Theoretical Definition	Theoretical Definition	Theoretical Definition	Composite Definition	Composite Definition
5	Protocol Validity	Protocol validity is whether an acceptable measurement protocol is adopted to ensure that a specific attribute on the entity is consistent and repeatable.	Dimensionless	Dimensionless	Dimensionless	Dimensionless	Dimensionless	Dimensionless	Dimensionless	Dimensionless
6	Appropriate Continuity	Valid indirect measures should not exhibit unexpected discontinuities; that is, they should be defined in all reasonable or expected situations. Thus, $Measure1 = Count1/Count2$, may present problems if $Count2 = 0$ (when Measure1 becomes infinity) or if $Count1 = 0$ (when Measure1 becomes zero)	NA	NA	NA	Numerator i.e. Earned Value (EV) can be zero if no activity is started against the WBS control accounts with respect to earning rules. Actual cost (AC) i.e. denominator can be zero if there are no costs accounted	Numerator i.e. Earned Value (EV) can be zero if no activity is started against the WBS control accounts with respect to earning rules. Planned Value (PV) i.e. denominator can be zero if the effort/cost and schedule is not estimated against the WBS Control Accounts.	Cpk is based on DPMO which in turn is dependent on the defects captured against every opportunity	Numerator can be zero before the "Testing" starts and defects are not captured. Denominator cannot be zero as every development will map to functionality/FPs	Numerator can be zero when the defects captured are not resolved. Denominator cannot be zero as every development will have some FPs which in turn can map to the total defects that can be possible in the system
7	Dimensional Consistency	A metric has dimensional consistency if the formulation of multiple metrics into a composite metric is performed by a scientifically well-understood mathematical function.	NA	NA	NA	Dimensional analysis on both sides of the equation is satisfied	Dimensional analysis on both sides of the equation is satisfied	Dimensional analysis on both sides of the equation is satisfied	Dimensional analysis on both sides of the equation is satisfied	Dimensional analysis on both sides of the equation is satisfied

The Kaner and Bond's ten validation questions are summarized below in table 51 [Kaner and Bond, 2004].

Table 51: Validating Measures using the Ten Questions

Sl # / Question\Measure	Lines of Code (LOC)	Function Points (FP)	McCabe's Cyclomatic Complexity (CC)	Schedule Performance Index (SPI)	Cost Performance Index (CPI)	Sigma Level (SL)	Defect Density (DD)	Defect Removal Efficiency (DRE)
1 What is the purpose of this measure i.e. what is it that we are trying to measure?	LOC is to measure the Size before development	FP is to measure the Size after development	CC counts the number of decision paths in the program	SPI shows the efficiency of the time utilized	CPI shows the efficiency of the utilization of budget	SL gives the effectiveness of the entire SDLC in the project	DD compares the number of defects in various software components	DRE provides the rate at which defects are resolved
2 What is the scope of this measure?	Size of the work after development	Size of the work before development	Maintenance including Testing	Schedule	Cost or Effort	Quality	Quality	Quality
3 What attribute are we trying to measure?	Size	Size	Complexity	Duration or Schedule	Cost or Effort	Process Variation	Stability	Speed or Time
4 What is the natural scale of the attribute we are trying to measure?	Ratio	Ratio	Interval	Ratio	Ratio	Ratio	Ratio	Ratio
5 What is the natural variability of the attribute?	Low	Medium	Low	Medium	Medium	Low	Medium	Medium
6 What measuring instrument do we use to perform the measurement?	Tools in the Development Environment	Combination of Eclipse plug-in & QSM Table	Eclipse plug-in	MS project or equivalent	MS project or equivalent	Sigma Conversion Table	Calculator	Calculator
7 What is the natural scale for this metric?	Ratio	Ratio	Interval	Ratio	Ratio	Ratio	Nominal	Nominal
8 What is the natural variability of readings from this instrument?	Low	Low	Low	Medium	Medium	Low	Low	Low
9 What is the relationship of the attribute to the metric value?	High	Medium	High	Medium	Medium	High	Medium	Low
10 What are the natural and foreseeable side effects of using this instrument?	Medium	Medium	Medium	Medium	Medium	Medium	Medium	Medium

5.3 Results of Empirical Validation

5.3.1 Results of Case Studies

The first project status report using the measurement framework was presented when the first iteration (the circled box in figure 24 in section 4.3.1.1) was completed. The status report is as shown in the table 52 below.

Table 52: Measurement Data after the First Iteration

Sr # FDD Name	Lines of Code (LDC)	Function Points FP	Total McCabe Complexity	Complexity Type	CPI	SPI	Total Test Cases (Opportunities)	Defects Open and untested Test Cases	DPMO	Sigma Level	DD	Total Defects possible	Defects Removed	DRE
1:PT_EH_01-Deposit & FDD Maintenance	2134	10	295	High	1.50	0.81	34	31	911765	0.35	3.08	18	2	0.17
2:PT_EH_01-LO-Deposit & FDD Maintenance - Change A/c Holder	1067	5	160	High	0.73	1.00	27	13	481481	1.55	7.61	27	14	0.52
3:PT_EH_04-Registered Plans & IFSA - Contract Details	2764	13	341	High	0.83	0.81	10	6	600000	1.25	9.46	24	4	0.16
4:PT_EH_05-Registered Plans & IFSA - Contract Maintenance	1728	8	371	High	1.00	0.94	24	20	833333	0.53	3.48	24	4	0.17
5:PT_EH_09-Loan - Account Details	865	4	117	High	1.30	0.92	20	4	200000	2.61	0.99	20	16	0.80
6:PT_EH_10,16,18-Loan - Make Payment + Lumpsum + Payout	2521	12	346	High	0.80	1.05	15	13	866667	0.39	1.10	22	2	0.09
7:PT_EH_14-Loan - Disbursement - Loan Maintenance	2064	10	367	High	1.00	1.03	20	16	800000	0.86	1.66	20	4	0.20
8:PT_EH_17-Loan - Payout Scenario - Loan Maintenance	1513	7	273	High	1.15	1.12	10	2	200000	2.34	0.28	12	8	0.66
9:PT_EH_26-View Restatements	1307	6	238	High	1.30	1.00	35	30	857143	4.02	4.91	35	5	0.14
10:PT_EH_26-Transfers	18603	87	1380	High	0.76	0.86	112	106	897436	0.23	1.21	265	12	0.05
11:PT_EH_26-Fees	2298	11	229	High	0.91	0.91	45	37	822222	0.58	3.45	45	6	0.18
12:PT_EH_27-Supervisor Overrides	1052	5	99	High	1.42	0.87	8	7	875000	0.35	1.45	7	1	0.14
13:PT_EH_32,33-Overdraft Protection Details & Maintenance	4671	22	641	High	1.53	0.95	45	41	911111	0.13	1.96	45	4	0.09
14:PT_EH_60-Deposit & FDD Account Details	1298	6	172	High	1.49	0.96	7	1	142857	2.57	0.16	19	6	0.63
15:PT_EH_61-Registered Plan Payments incl Close Accounts	10107	47	1216	High	1.39	0.97	100	91	910000	0.16	1.93	124	6	0.07
16:PT_EH_62-Deposits - Close Accounts	1620	8	357	High	1.69	1.00	26	14	538462	2.57	1.85	26	12	0.46
17:PT_EH_64-FDD Funding for Non-Registered Products	2094	10	271	High	0.69	0.87	17	14	823529	0.57	1.42	17	3	0.17
Overall	57506	269	6704	High	1.01	0.94	360	445	794643	0.68	1.66	781	113	0.16

The final project status report is as shown in the table 53 below.

Table 53: Measurement Data after the Final Iteration

Project Status as on July 31st, 2010 (Project Ending; All three iterations completed)

Sl #	FDD Name	Lines of Code (LOC)	Function Points (FP)	Total McCabe Complexity	Complexity Type	CPI	SPI	Total Test Cases (Opportunities)	Defects Open incl unresolved Test Cases	DPMO	Sigma Level	DD	Total Defects	Defects Removed	DRE
1	PT_EH_01-Deposit & FDD Maintenance	2290	11	309	High	1.15	1.00	34	2	58824	3.07	0.18	34	32	0.94
2	PT_EH_01-0-Deposit & FDD Maintenance - Change A/c Holder	1195	6	155	High	0.79	1.00	27	2	74074	2.95	0.36	27	25	0.93
3	PT_EH_04-Registered Plans & TFSA - Contract Details	2988	14	341	High	0.68	1.00	10	1	100000	2.78	0.07	27	7	0.26
4	PT_EH_05-Registered Plans & TFSA - Contract Maintenance	1793	8	394	High	1.11	1.00	24	2	83333	2.88	0.24	24	19	0.79
5	PT_EH_09-Loan - Account Details	971	5	126	High	1.30	1.00	20	1	50000	3.15	0.22	20	18	0.90
6	PT_EH_10_16_18-Loan - Make Payment + Lumpsum + Payout	2630	12	370	High	0.86	1.00	15	2	133333	2.61	0.16	23	14	0.62
7	PT_EH_14-Loan - Disbursement - Loan Maintenance	2183	10	353	High	1.00	1.00	20	8	400000	1.75	0.78	20	12	0.60
8	PT_EH_17-Loan - Payout Scenario - Loan Maintenance	1343	7	291	High	0.96	1.00	10	3	300000	2.02	0.42	12	7	0.59
9	PT_EH_20-View Estatements	1307	6	243	High	1.63	1.00	35	3	85714	2.87	0.49	35	32	0.91
10	PT_EH_24-Transfers	18841	88	1494	High	1.10	1.00	117	2	17094	3.62	0.02	270	115	0.43
11	PT_EH_26-Fees	2336	11	241	High	0.95	1.00	45	12	266667	2.12	1.10	45	33	0.73
12	PT_EH_27-Supervisor Overrides	1167	5	104	High	1.35	1.00	32	12	375000	1.82	2.20	32	20	0.63
13	PT_EH_32_33-Overdraft Protection Details & Maintenance	4982	23	687	High	1.30	1.00	45	9	200000	2.34	0.39	51	33	0.65
14	PT_EH_60-Deposit & FDD Account Details	1419	7	183	High	1.65	1.00	7	1	142857	2.57	0.15	11	6	0.56
15	PT_EH_61-Registered Plan Payments incl Close Accounts	10724	50	1426	High	1.30	1.00	120	25	208333	2.31	0.50	133	95	0.71
16	PT_EH_62-Deposits - Close Accounts	1643	8	212	High	1.87	1.00	26	2	76923	2.93	0.26	26	24	0.92
17	PT_EH_64-FDD Funding for Non Registered Products	2241	10	289	High	1.00	1.00	17	1	58824	3.07	0.19	39	15	0.80
	Overall	60322	282	7218	High	1.04	1.00	624	88	141026	2.58	0.31	808	490	0.61

Figure 35 below shows improvement in the overall project status between the first status report and the final status report.

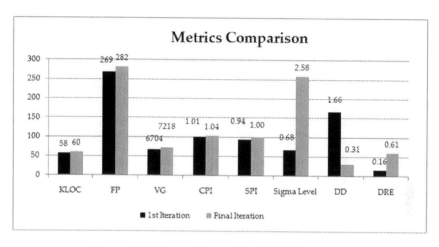

Figure 35: Comparison of the Eight Measures

Significant improvements are on Cpk, DD and DRE measures indicating improvements in the project quality. The increase in Cpk shows improvement in the SDLC process due to reduced defects. The reduction in DD indicates increase in product stability while the increase in DRE shows improvement in the rate at which defects are resolved. This satisfies the two remaining criteria for empirical validation:

- **Discriminative power.** For the eight measures, the critical threshold value for SPI and CPI is anything less than one, while the project benchmarks for Cpk was at 2.0, DD was at 0.5 and DRE was at 0.5.
- **Trackability.** This criterion is used to assess whether a component is improving, degrading, or stagnating in quality over time. For example, Cpk, DD and DRE are shown to be trackable, as fixing the defects increases the quality in the project.

The primary success criteria for the **initiators and implementers** is that - a successful project is one that is completed within 10% of its committed cost and schedule and has delivered all of its intended functions [Humphrey, 2005]. In this project, the tracking was against the base-lined plan for which the metrics were presented after the first iteration of "Requirements-Development-Testing" was completed. Accordingly, the projected schedule at completion = Initial Duration/SPI = 6/0.94 = 6.38 Months and the projected cost at completion = Initial Budgeted Cost/CPI = 1520/1.01 = 1504 Person-days (PDs). When the project was completed on 31st July, the schedule at Completion = Initial Duration/SPI = 6/1.00 = 6 Months while the Cost at Completion = Initial Budgeted Cost/CPI = 1520 /1.04 = 1462 PDs. So both the schedule and cost were within 10% of the committed cost and schedule for the agreed scope.

In addition the primary success criteria for the **beneficiaries** are based on two parameters.

a. **Defect rate according to CMMI levels.**

This project was managed according to CMMI level 3 standards (i.e. defined business process) where the standards, process descriptions, and procedures were tailored from the organization's set of standard processes to suit this particular project. For a CMMI level 3 organization the defect rate should be 0.27 defects per FP [Kan, 2003]. This translates to 77 defects for the 282 FPs in scope for this project (77 = 282 * 0.27) and this number i.e. 77 is close to the 88 defects still open to be resolved as shown in table 52. So as far as the user's primary concern of quality is concerned, the existing defect count when the project is completed meets their requirements as it is close to SEI CMMI Level 3 standards.

b. **DRE levels**

According to David Longstreet, a software project is mature if the DRE is greater than 45% [Longstreet, 2008] and this project meets the standard as the DRE was 61%.

It is not practical to bring the defect count to zero in any project and this always invites discussion if it is feasible to achieve such a goal. In this project, these two defect criteria values (the defect rate of 88 defects and DRE of 61%) were acceptable to all stakeholders in the project as the strategy was to deploy the application along with other dependent application on a particular date. Moreover the must-have functionalities in the project were defect free and regression tested.

The eight measures were used to regularly present the project status every week. The weekly status reporting helped the stakeholders track the project objectively and make corrective actions on scheduling (Fast Tracking, Crashing and Resource Leveling), budgeting, buffer management et cetera for successful project completion. Measuring the reliability of the measurement data/instrument was unnecessary because the measurement model was objective relying on one data infrastructure. Some of the corrective actions taken in the project based on the eight measures were:

- Increased testing and assigning highly skilled developers (with focus on effective defect resolution) for bigger sized and more complexity functions. For example, Transfers functionality based on the first iteration report.
- Functions with poor DRE and low SPI (Example is PT_EH_04 – Registered Plans & TFSA – Contract Details where the DRE was 0.09 and SPI was 1.05 after the first iteration) functions were put on the "Max-Attention" list.
- Functions with low sigma levels and low complexity/size/SPI were prioritized due to their "Low-hanging fruit" status.
- Impact analysis was primarily driven from FPs. For instance after every iteration of "Requirements-Development-Testing" for every increase/decrease of one FP, approximately 125 LOC were also factored and other measures were derived for complete impact.

While the objective of the case studies (controlled and uncontrolled) was primarily empirically validation, the case studies threw some interesting light on the implementation aspects of measurement frameworks. More than a technical exercise, the implementation of the measurement framework was an organizational initiative involving people, process and technology. Below are some important lessons learned during the implementation of the measurement model in the two projects.

- As measures are meant for tracking the project delivery, train and educate the project team on how the project progress is tracked for their inclusiveness in the measurement program.
- When making decisions with these measures, consider the trend over multiple time periods. The Trend analysis can be used not only to predict future values but also to calculate expected values for comparison to actual current values.
- Be sensitive to the fact that improving one measure may cause another measure to deteriorate. For instances concentrating on improving the quality measures, might adversely impact the schedule.
- Use one standard format of the status report and assign the responsibility of the status report to the Project Manager as multiple formats from different sources lead to multiple interpretations.
- Recognize the business situation surrounding the measures and use measures to get the direction needed to accomplish the project goals.
- Decision making with schedule and cost measures is usually easy and incomplete. Collecting and analyzing quality measures are difficult and they invariably have lot of "information" on project status.
- Understand the "culture" and "acceptance" of these measures in the project.
- Though metrics are expensive and time consuming to define, collect, analyze and report; only the first status report takes significant time. The subsequent status reports take much less time.
- Finally, be sensitive to people's aspirations and their situations in the project. Do not measure or compare people with measures.

Metrics essentially provide the foundation and rationale for decision making.

5.3.2 Results of the Survey

To summarize, the survey presents following key pieces of information:

1. 74% of the respondents accept that the above eight measures can serve as a core set for an objective status of a software project. The remaining 26% were either neutral (rated 3 i.e. neutral) or were disagreed (response was 1 or 2) that the eight measures can serve as a core set.

    As mentioned in chapter 3, Net Promoter Score (NPS) rating between 50% to 80% is considered good [Reichheld, 2003]. The survey response data provided the NPS scores as shown below in figure 36 where the dark line shows the 50% threshold for NPS efficiency. Except LOC, the remaining seven measures were promoted by the industry practititioners.

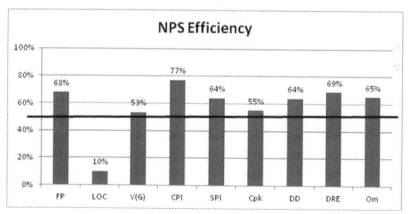

Figure 36: NPS Efficiency

2. As shown in above the NPS efficiency chart, LOC is the weakest of the eight measures with NPS efficiency at 10%. However LOC will be included in the measurement model for:

- It has been extensively and routinely used in the industry [Fenton, 2006].
- Will be always used in association with Function Points (FP).

3. The survey addresses three of the seven empirical validation criteria. They are repeatability, association, and predictability.
   A. Summary of Repeatability Validation Criteria

The Pearson's correlation for all the measures between the pilot test and the final survey response was close to the recommended threshold value of 0.90 satisfying the **repeatability criteria** for empirical validation [Schneidewind, 1992]. In addition, the overall value of Cronbach's alpha was found to be 0.78 which again exceeded the threshold of 0.70 set for **repeatability criteria** for reliability/repeatability [Schneidewind, 1992].

B. Summary of Association Validation Criteria

The **association** validity criteria states that — a measure has association validity if it has a direct, linear statistical correlation with an external quality factor which in this case is the Overall Measure (Om). The below table 54 shows that except for the association between FP and Om, there is association between the other seven measures and Om.

Table 54: Summary of Association Validation Criteria

Measure	Pearson's Correlation	P-value from 2-tailed test	Inference
FP	0.15	0.11	Accept Ho.
LOC	0.29	0.00	Reject Ho
V(G)	0.36	0.00	Reject Ho
CPI	0.21	0.03	Reject Ho
SPI	0.25	0.01	Reject Ho
Cpk	0.41	0.00	Reject Ho
DD	0.31	0.00	Reject Ho
DRE	0.19	0.05	Reject Ho

A. Summary of Predictability Validation Criteria

The regression model has 45.3% of the variability (Value of R-square is 0.4528) in the dependent variable (i.e. Om) explained in the regression model. Here the value of R^2 i.e. goodness of fit is close to 0.5 illustrating a good amount of **predictably.**

4. There is no difference or relationship in the way the stakeholders see the software project measurement except for LOC. There is also no relationship/difference in the way the stakeholders see the LOC and FP measures. But the stakeholders see the Earned Value Management (EVM) measures (i.e. SPI and CPI) and the quality measures (Cpk, DD and DRE) differently.

5.4 Contribution to Body of Knowledge (BoK)

The results from the empirical validation show that the proposed measurement model with the eight measures can be successfully applied in software projects. The specific benefits from this research including novel contribution to the software metrics and software portfolio project management (SPPM) body of knowledge (BoK) can be sub-divided into two areas.

1. BoK pertaining to the construction of the Measurement Model
2. BoK pertaining to the Validation of the Measurement Model

Measurement Model

*   B1: It meets the value propositions of all direct software project stakeholders during the project duration. Understanding stakeholders' needs and expectations is crucial to the success of the software project including the measurement program. According to Rad and Levin, stakeholder needs reflecting the overall project success must be captured in through the measures [Rad and Levin, 2005].

- B2: Measures bring objectivity as thresholds, variances and control limits can be set for improved decision making in the project. It improves decision making as it relies on measures. This helps to determine if established standards, goals and acceptance criteria are being met so that suitable corrective actions can be taken. In addition, the list of 204 questions based on the stakeholder needs that any software projects can be used as a ready reckoner checklist to audit the status of a software project.
- B3: It is cost effective as the measures are proven, available in most commercial tools, quick and easy to derive. According to Delone and Mclean, despite the multidimensional and contingent nature of Information systems (IS), an attempt should be made to reduce significantly the number of measures used to measure IS success [Delone and Mclean, 2003]. Having a small set of measures avoids confusion, micromanagement and eventually paralysis not only of the measurement program but also of the software project. In addition, human beings can typically cope with 7 ± 2 pieces of information at a time [Miller, 1957]. According to Jim Clemmer, "The key to effective measurement is a small number of simple measures that channel the organization's energy and focus on the strategic areas with the highest potential return" [Clemmer, 1992]. Also Patrik Berander and Per Jönsson recommend that, having too many measurements to collect and analyze might imply that no measurements are used at all [Berander and Jönsson, 2006]. Hence the measurement model should have a small number of measures.

Validation

- B5: The model developed is practical. It is implemented in a real world business critical project where the project was regularly tracked for successful completion.
- B6: It is empirical validated as the measurement model was assessed by over 123 seasoned practitioners who brought

over 2000 years of global software project experience from multiple industries from 32 countries.

- B7: It offers a set of 14 generic validation criteria where a hybrid or bespoke software project measurement model can be validated.

5.5 Conclusion

The research results show that the measurement model can be successfully implemented in a real world project satisfying all the validation criteria. Given the time taken to implement a reasonably big project (greater than 300 FPs and 6 month duration), the survey provided diversity by providing responses from 123 industry practitioners from 32 countries sharing close to 2000 years of their software project experience. While the rigor in research and the tools used to analyze might enhance the validity and reliability, the measurement model is still based on a few assumptions and still has limitations. The next chapter lists the assumptions and addresses the limitations and for a more robust measurement model for software projects.

Chapter 6

Conclusion

6.1 Introduction

Software project management involves making critical decisions based on different parameters at different SDLC phases. Hence the proposed GQM based measurement model with eight measures can help stakeholders identify key events and trends thereby making informed and rational decisions. Though the measurement model is scientifically derived and validated theoretically and empirically, it has a set of assumptions, limitations and delimitations. While the delimitations were covered in chapter1, this chapter looks at the assumptions and limitations in the implementation and usage of the measurement model.

6.2 Assumptions in this Research

An assumption is basically a realistic expectation. Along with the theoretical and empirical validation criteria, the below assumptions further enhance the applicability of the measurement model. The key assumptions here are:

- The data collected in the case study and survey is unbiased and un-manipulated.
- The stakeholders are committed to the successful implementation of the measurement model.

- The tools and process to capture the relevant data on the eight measurers is available in the project.
- While Inferential statistical analysis techniques either explain or predict the relationship between one or more variables, an exact causal connection can never be absolutely determined. Statistical analysis provides only explanatory or predictive utility. Hence a level of confidence, expressed as a probability of error (p value), is used for the explanation of the relationship between variables.
- The sample size used in the empirical validation is a representative of the population of the software project stakeholders and the sample respondents used might not accurately reflect the total population.
- The stakeholders in the project have the right roles and responsibilities and play a single unique role.

6.3 Limitations of this Research

The eight measures proposed are not the golden measures. Depending on the project needs more measures including requirements volatility and risk can be added or measures such as LOC (which has low NPS score in the survey) can even be dropped. However though every software project is unique, it still shares some generic and common characteristics with other software projects. Hence a generic core set of measures to report the software project status should work when a suite of key measures is common, popular and successful in many other industry sectors where decision-making is typically constrained by the lack of information and time. For example:

- In economics, the prosperity index of countries is based on 89 variables grouped into eight categories namely economy, entrepreneurship/opportunity, governance, education, health, safety/security, personal freedom and social capital
- In stock markets, there are ten ratios to assess the financial health of the company in three areas namely [Chen and Shimerda, 1981]:

1. Profitability

    a. Gross Margin Percentage,
    b. Sales, General and Administrative expense %
    c. Operating Margin
    d. Return on Sales

2. Efficiency

    a. Inventory turn-over
    b. Days Sales Outstanding
    c. Asset Turnover

3. Capital Management

    a. Current Ratio
    b. Quick Ratio
    c. Leverage Ratio

- In health care, treatment, therapeutic trials and clinical studies on many ailments are conducted using a core set of measures with appropriate indicators.
- Supply Chain Operations Reference (SCOR) has identified thirteen measures to monitor overall supply chain performance.
- The "APGAR" score to assess the health of newborn children is determined using five simple criteria - Appearance, Pulse, Grimace, Activity, and Respiration.
- In sports, the winner of the Olympic decathlon is acknowledged as the world's finest athlete.
- Closer to this subject, there is the six metrics suite "MOOSE" (Metrics for Object-Oriented Software Engineering) proposed by Chidamber and Kemerer. These six metrics are:

1. Weighted methods per class (WMC)
2. Depth of inheritance (DIT)
3. Number of direct sub-classes (NOC)
4. Coupling between object classes (CBO)

5. Response set for a class(RFC)
6. Lack of cohesion in methods (LCOM)

While we can debate the inclusion of more measures to the list of software project measures at additional costs citing different contexts, these core eight measures are meant to be a minimum set capturing critical information most relevant to the stakeholders. The project reporting can start with this core set, derive some value and then expand if necessary depending on unique project needs and circumstances. For example, the product manager might want to have more granularities on v (G) for product stability. In that case perhaps cohesion and coupling (between software components) related measures as sub-metrics under v (G) might provide additional information.

However empirical validation (i.e. the two case studies and the survey) have provided some key factors which will increase the possibility of successfully implementing the proposed measurement model.

Product Factors

- **Project Type.** As mentioned in the hypothesis section in chapter 2, the measures for the software project are for Bespoke and Hybrid-COTS development projects. These measures are not designed for software maintenance or COTS type of projects.
- **Size.** As FPs calculation is labor-intensive and expensive for applications greater than 15,000 FPs [Jones, 2002], this measurement framework works well for applications/projects less than 15,000 FPs. (An application greater than 15,000 FPs can be categorized as a program and broken down into smaller projects for better control and management.)

Process Factors

- **Realistic PMB.** Requirements should be complete, correct and non-volatile. Based on this, the effort estimate (for planned value in EVM) should be done rationally and the project should be baselined for the measurements can be carried out against this baseline.

- **Mature data collection infrastructure.** Given that measurement programs are expensive and time consuming to define, collect, report and analyze the measurement data collection infrastructure (Tools and Methodology) should be available for the data to be collected regularly and made readily available at all times. This is generally found in SEI CMMI level 3 organizations and higher.
- **Regular Application.** Hence the measurement framework should be applied regularly and frequently in every phase of the SDLC. This improves the feedback process and ultimately the project delivery.

Resource Factors

- **Stakeholder commitment.** The project stakeholders should be committed to the measurement program. Every stakeholder from the developer to the tester to the senior management should actively participate in the measurement process to make it successful.

6.4 Future Research

The results of both the literature review and the research findings suggest directions for future research concerning software project metrics. Future research based on the proposed measurement model and the validation criteria can involve work in the following areas for increased reliability of the measurement framework:

1. GQM+
2. Requirements engineering
3. EVM Earning rules
4. Process Complexity

Research Area 1- GQM+

The success of a measurement initiative in a software company depends on the quality of the links between metrics programs and organizational business goals. However in chapter 3, we started with the derivation of the measures with the project goal s of the stakeholders assuming that the project goals of stakeholders are aligned to the organizational business goals. However this is an assumption and one of the disadvantages of GQM paradigm could be the misalignment of organizational business goals and project measures. In this circumstance, GQM+ strategies is an extension to GQM which adds the capability to create measurement programs that ensure alignment between business goals and strategies, software specific goals and measurement.

Research Area 2- Requirements Engineering

A dominant reason for failure in a software project has been attributed to requirements as requirements drive almost every project activity in the SDLC such as scoping, estimating/ budgeting, scheduling, coding, testing, documentation and training. "Clear Statement of Requirements" is at #3 in the list of critical factors from Standish Group that make software projects successful [Standish, 2009]. A controlled study by SEI found that the most important factor for project success was the way the project team did its "requirements elicitation and management" [Woody, 2005]. Hence a measurement model/framework to specifically address the challenges in the requirements phase will help the stakeholders to take remedial actions early in the project.

Research Area 3 - Earning Rules

The standard earning rules in EVM are closely associated with the NDIA (National Defense Industrial Association) ANSI/EIA (American National Standards Institute /Electronics Industries Alliance)-748 standards which contain 32 criteria drawn from five process areas [Budd and Budd, 2005]. These earning rules and criteria are more suited for a production floor set up where the relationship between output and input is linear, predictable and visible unlike software projects. The earning rules and the criteria need to be revalidated for sufficiency, appropriateness and relevancy for software projects.

Research Area 4 – Process Complexity

Complexity in a project exists in product, process and resources. Some are standalone while many more interact with each other. While the product or technical complexity is addressed with McCabe's cyclomatic complexity, to understand the process and resource complexity the research has to encompass cognitive sciences (an interdisciplinary scientific study of information concerning faculties such as perception, language, reasoning, and emotion).

6.5 Conclusion

Science thrives on measurement and in any scientific field measurement generates quantitative descriptions of key products, processes and resources. With appropriate measurement model we can clarify and understand the issues better and take suitable corrective actions.

This enhanced understanding helps to select better techniques and tools to control and improve the software project delivery. Hence a good measurement framework not only provides the information for improvement but also acts like a catalyst in improving the project visibility, and eventually attaining the project goals.

Good software project management demands a handful of validated measures which are regularly applied to gauge the health of a project. The eight measures are meant to be minimum-set to increase the odds of knowing the project status holistically and to complete the project successfully. Apart from providing vital information on the project performance, the measurement framework can also serve as the basis for clear and objective communication with project stakeholders, promote teamwork and improve team morale by linking efforts of individual team members to the project goals. Finally, there is no engineering without measurement and software engineering can become a true engineering discipline if we build a solid foundation of measurement-based theories [Pfleeger et al, 1997].

Appendix 1

204 Questions to the Project Stakeholders

#	Project Sub-entity	Stakeholder type	Dimension	Question
1	Product	Initiator	Data	What are the key deliverables that are needed to accomplish the project goal?
2	Product	Initiator	Data	How is the data conceptualized in the Entity Relationship diagram (ERD)?
3	Product	Initiator	Function	What is to be accomplished from the project?
4	Product	Initiator	Function	How are the product constraints (more applicable for COTS and Hybrid COTS) addressed?
5	Product	Initiator	Function	What are Business processes addressed by the product?
6	Product	Initiator	Function	Is the implementation adhering to regulatory and compliance standards?
6	Product	Initiator	Function	How is the TCO and ROI on the project realized?
7	Product	Initiator	Network	What are the physical locations where the product will be used?

8	Product	Initiator	People	What are the business organizations where this product is needed?
9	Product	Initiator	People	Are appropriate stakeholders involved in the project?
10	Product	Initiator	People	Is there clearly one person responsible for managing the project?
11	Product	Initiator	People	Are requirements being provided any relevant business focal?
12	Product	Initiator	Time	What is the list of key business events?
13	Product	Initiator	Motivation	Are the items important to the Project motivated by the business goals?
14	Product	Initiator	Motivation	What are the signs that indicate that project may fail?
15	Product	Implementer	Data	Is the Data Model normalized with smaller tables and well-structured relations?
16	Product	Implementer	Data	Is the Data Architecture entities are converted to table definitions, object classes, hierarchy segments, or whatever is appropriate in line with the DBMS to be used.
17	Product	Implementer	Data	Is the table space designed well?
18	Product	Implementer	Data	Is UTF-8 used for Databases, Tables, connections, Strings et cetera.?
19	Product	Implementer	Data	Are disk packs appropriately are allocated?
20	Product	Implementer	Data	What are the System, Master and transactional data?
21	Product	Implementer	Data	How is error/exception handling addressed?

22	Product	Implementer	Data	If there are interfaces, are the necessary data format specifications, API documentations all collected?
23	Product	Implementer	Function	Is the Stakeholder Analysis carried out?
24	Product	Implementer	Function	Is the Business Process Model (BPM) developed?
25	Product	Implementer	Function	How does the Data flow diagram (DFD) showing the transformation of input data into output data look like?
26	Product	Implementer	Function	Is the System Design where the output to a UML output or a pseudo code available?
27	Product	Implementer	Function	Is the detailed program design including the source and object codes designed?
28	Product	Implementer	Function	How are the business functions translated to the code level?
29	Product	Beneficiary	Function	How complex is the application?
30	Product	Implementer	Function	What is the stability of requirements?
31	Product	Implementer	Network	How will the various locations interact with each other?
32	Product	Implementer	Network	Are all forms validated for consistency on the client and server side?
33	Product	Implementer	Network	Is the Architecture for data distribution defined including itemizing what information is created where and where it is to be used?
34	Product	Implementer	Network	What is the System Architecture including hardware, software et cetera.

35	Product	Implementer	Network	Network Architecture such as hardware, protocols, communications facilities et cetera.?
36	Product	Implementer	Network	How is the System Landscape formulated?
37	Product	Implementer	People	Is the Org chart with roles and responsibilities defined for software use?
38	Product	Implementer	People	Is the Human-Computer Interaction (HCI) architecture specifically in terms of who needs what information designed?
39	Product	Implementer	Time	When are the functions invoked and under what circumstances?
40	Product	Implementer	Time	Is there a dependency diagram including and entity state changes?
41	Product	Implementer	Time	Is there a Control flow diagram encompassing program triggers and messages?
42	Product	Implementer	Time	What is the timing definition including job scheduling?
43	Product	Implementer	Motivation	What are the assumptions and constraints that are applicable here?
44	Product	Implementer	Motivation	How are the business rules converted into program design elements?
45	Product	Implementer	Motivation	How are the business rules specified in program logic?
46	Product	Beneficiary	Data	How is the data converted from the legacy application?
47	Product	Beneficiary	Data	What are the data handling equipment/procedures that should be used to process, compile, analyze, and transmit data reliably and accurately?

48	Product	Beneficiary	Data	How is the data integrity ensured?
49	Product	Beneficiary	Data	What are the process for data archival and retrieval?
50	Product	Beneficiary	Function	Is the application mature and stable?
51	Product	Beneficiary	Function	Is the Code linked and converted to executable programs?
52	Product	Beneficiary	Function	Is the code sufficiently commented?
53	Product	Beneficiary	Network	What Communications facilities are needed?
54	Product	Beneficiary	People	Is the User Interface design aspects such as interface graphics, navigation paths, security rules and presentation style
55	Product	Beneficiary	People	How will the users be trained on the new software?
56	Product	Beneficiary	Time	Are the businesses events respond as designed?
57	Product	Beneficiary	Motivation	How are the business rules enforced?
58	Process	Initiator	Integration Management	What are the show-stopper functions in the project?
59	Process	Initiator	Integration Management	Are the key deliverables completed as promised in the SOW/Contract?
60	Process	Initiator	Integration Management	How to manage changes?
61	Process	Initiator	Integration Management	Are all activities of the Project formally terminated?
62	Process	Initiator	Integration Management	Is software product handled over to the maintenance team with appropriate Knowledge transfer?

63	Process	Initiator	Integration Management	Are all the Project resources released?
64	Process	Initiator	Integration Management	Is the project de-briefing document created and signed off?
65	Process	Initiator	Integration Management	Are all the Project Documentation archived?
66	Process	Initiator	Integration Management	What kind of release management practices to follow?
67	Process	Initiator	Integration Management	Who will take responsibility for maintaining the application after go-live/deployment?
68	Process	Initiator	Integration Management	Does the project deliverables have any dependencies or conflicts with any other projects/programs/portfolios currently being run within the organization?
69	Process	Initiator	Integration Management	Is there a PMO which coordinates and centralizes the project management activities and functions?
70	Process	Implementer	Integration Management	What the dependencies of the tasks with other deliverables within the project?
71	Process	Initiator	Integration Management	Are some of the works delivered remotely?
72	Process	Initiator	Scope Management	Is the baselined scope as per the contract?
73	Process	Initiator	Time Management	How much time is needed to meet the scope/deliverables?
74	Process	Implementer	Time Management	What is schedule variance?
75	Process	Initiator	Cost Management	How much money is needed to meet the scope/deliverables?

76	Process	Implementer	Cost Management	What is effort variance?
77	Process	Initiator	Cost Management	How are unnecessary activities (waste) eliminated?
78	Process	Initiator	Cost Management	What is the productivity in the project?
79	Process	Initiator	Cost Management	Are costs being reconciled against corporate accounts?
80	Process	Initiator	Quality Management	What is the acceptable defects that can be carried over to the maintenance team?
81	Process	Initiator	Quality Management	How is the project conforming to the organizations quality standards/levels?
82	Process	Initiator	Quality Management	How are the Project reviews and audits carried out?
83	Process	Implementer	Human Resource Management	What is the Type of Project organization (Functional or Matrix or Projectized)
84	Process	Implementer	Human Resource Management	Is the project Org structure defined and communicated?
85	Process	Initiator	Human Resource Management	Do we have the appropriate amount of leadership commitment and oversight to ensure project delivery?
86	Process	Initiator	Communications Management	Are the right stakeholders being informed of the project progress?
87	Process	Initiator	Communications Management	Is there a regular project team meeting?
88	Process	Initiator	Risk Management	How are risks and/or issues addressed on a ongoing basis?
89	Process	Initiator	Risk Management	When should a risk be avoided/accepted/ mitigated/transferred?

90	Process	Initiator	Risk Management	Is this project a first of a kind for the vendor, either due to line of business, technical features, software releases or the like?
91	Process	Initiator	Procurement Management	Have we identified any other "part-time" or transient resources required for project delivery?
92	Process	Initiator	Procurement Management	What other similar external services have been rendered?
93	Process	Initiator	Procurement Management	Is there a global contract with the vendor that can be leveraged?
94	Process	Initiator	Procurement Management	What are the Vendor evaluation criteria?
95	Process	Initiator	Procurement Management	What security access will the vendor resources permitted to?
96	Process	Initiator	Procurement Management	In a multi-vendor scenario how is the relationship amongst different vendors?
97	Process	Initiator	Procurement Management	Is there a recognized project life cycle toll gate deliverables including formal authorization to start the next phase?
98	Process	Implementer	Integration Management	How is the project plan developed?
99	Process	Implementer	Integration Management	Who approves the integrated project plan?
100	Process	Implementer	Integration Management	Is the project formally closed with a sign-off and closure document?
101	Process	Implementer	Integration Management	What is the size of the project?
102	Process	Implementer	Integration Management	Top-down planning estimates created

103	Process	Implementer	Integration Management	Do we have relevant templates and checklists for project execution?
104	Process	Implementer	Integration Management	What is the project type - COTS/Hybrid/Bespoke?
105	Process	Implementer	Integration Management	What is the development methodology to be used?
106	Process	Implementer	Integration Management	What are the approvals to re-baseline the project?
107	Process	Implementer	Integration Management	What is the criterion under which the Change Control Board approves or rejects change requests?
108	Process	Implementer	Integration Management	Who issues the project charter?
109	Process	Implementer	Integration Management	What is the Contingency Reserve/buffer available?
110	Process	Implementer	Integration Management	How is the effort estimation (Top-down and bottom-up) done?
111	Process	Implementer	Integration Management	What is the criteria to approve the project plan?
112	Process	Implementer	Integration Management	What are the entry and exit criteria for Unit testing, Assembly testing and Integration testing?
113	Process	Implementer	Integration Management	What are the Naming and coding standards to be followed?
114	Process	Implementer	Integration Management	What are the key artifacts needed in a project?
115	Process	Implementer	Integration Management	How is the project measured/tracked?
116	Process	Implementer	Integration Management	Are proper signed authorities in place for key decisions?
117	Process	Implementer	Integration Management	Is Earned Value Management used?

118	Process	Implementer	Scope Management	How and when is the WBS baselined (Scope, Time and Cost)?
119	Process	Implementer	Scope Management	How is the Work Performance Measurement done?
120	Process	Implementer	Scope Management	Is the scope baselined?
121	Process	Implementer	Scope Management	Is the scope creeping/ volatile?
122	Process	Implementer	Time Management	Is the project activity relationships defined?
123	Process	Implementer	Time Management	What is the acceptable float?
124	Process	Implementer	Time Management	Are milestones being used to manage progress?
125	Process	Implementer	Time Management	Is time being monitored through a time sheeting system?
126	Process	Implementer	Time Management	Is there a solid and realistic plan for the remaining work?
127	Process	Implementer	Cost Management	What is the budget plan?
128	Process	Implementer	Quality Management	What is the quality plan?
129	Process	Implementer	Quality Management	Is the test plan realistic (test strategy, test plan and test cases in place)?
130	Process	Implementer	Quality Management	Is data available for validating the requirements?
131	Process	Implementer	Quality Management	What is the scope of regression testing?
132	Process	Implementer	Quality Management	What are the Quality standards/CMMI levels of the project?
133	Process	Implementer	Quality Management	What is the defect definition?

134	Process	Implementer	Quality Management	How are test cases formulated?
135	Process	Implementer	Quality Management	How are issues tracked and resolved?
136	Process	Implementer	Quality Management	Are all the items (use cases, et cetera.) atomic, and (where possible) measureable?
137	Process	Implementer	Quality Management	What actions happen after a quality review, and are they monitored?
138	Process	Implementer	Quality Management	Is proper version control in place?
139	Process	Implementer	Human Resource Management	Who are the positive and negative stakeholders in the project?
140	Process	Implementer	Human Resource Management	What is the staffing plan to onboard and roll-off resources?
141	Process	Implementer	Human Resource Management	Do you enough skilled resources in the project?
142	Process	Implementer	Human Resource Management	Is the team motivated to work in the project?
143	Process	Implementer	Human Resource Management	What stage of team building is the team in (Forming/Storming/Forming/Performing?
144	Process	Implementer	Human Resource Management	Is the roles and responsibilities of the team defined and communicated?
145	Process	Implementer	Human Resource Management	What is the on boarding process for a new team member?

146	Process	Implementer	Human Resource Management	Is there a training plan in place?
147	Process	Implementer	Communications Management	Is there a communication plan?
148	Process	Implementer	Communications Management	Is there a project glossary?
149	Process	Implementer	Communications Management	Is there a decision register?
150	Process	Implementer	Communications Management	Is there a project team rooster?
151	Process	Implementer	Communications Management	Are the project artifacts accessible to the project stakeholders?
152	Process	Implementer	Risk Management	What is the risk management plan
153	Process	Implementer	Risk Management	How do you track risks?
154	Process	Implementer	Risk Management	How long can the contingency arrangements last?
155	Process	Implementer	Procurement Management	What is the procurement plan?
156	Process	Implementer	Procurement Management	Is the Contract/Purchase Order issued/signed?
157	Process	Implementer	Procurement Management	What is the type of contract - cost reimbursable and fixed price?
158	Process	Beneficiary	Integration Management	How will the new software be integrated into the enterprise application suite?
159	Process	Beneficiary	Integration Management	How will the software communicate with external applications from 3rd part vendors?
160	Process	Beneficiary	Integration Management	Is the relevant project documentation complete?

161	Process	Beneficiary	Scope Management	How is the traceability analysis carried out?
162	Process	Beneficiary	Time Management	Is the cut-over from the old to the new application on schedule?
163	Process	Beneficiary	Cost Management	What are the travel policies in the project?
164	Process	Beneficiary	Quality Management	How extensive is the testing carried out?
165	Process	Beneficiary	Quality Management	How is the FURPS testing of the application?
166	Process	Beneficiary	Quality Management	How is the code release carried out?
167	Process	Beneficiary	Quality Management	How quickly are the defects resolved?
168	Process	Beneficiary	Quality Management	How is the severity of the defects managed?
169	Process	Beneficiary	Quality Management	Is the project using source control?
170	Process	Beneficiary	Quality Management	Was the new code tested (and automated tests run) before committing?
171	Process	Beneficiary	Quality Management	Were the development features (error/exception display, default passwords, et cetera) deactivated in the deployed code?
172	Process	Beneficiary	Human Resource Management	What will be the effectiveness of the change management process?
173	Process	Beneficiary	Human Resource Management	How will the project impact my job?
174	Process	Beneficiary	Communications Management	How will the change communicated?
175	Process	Beneficiary	Risk Management	What are the current risk levels?

176	Process	Beneficiary	Procurement Management	What are the terms and conditions in the post deployment support from the vendor?
177	Resources	Initiator	People	Are the project Team members committed and engaged to the project?
178	Resources	Initiator	People	Is the post-deployment support plan ready?
179	Resources	Initiator	People	For how long the vendor resources be retained after go-live?
180	Resources	Initiator	People	Are skills such as empathy, creativity, group facilitation and influence apparent in the project team?
181	Resources	Implementer	People	How to handle non-productive team members?
182	Resources	Implementer	People	What did I learn from the project?
183	Resources	Implementer	People	How to handle project attrition?
184	Resources	Implementer	People	Is there a overtime allowance in the project?
185	Resources	Beneficiary	People	Will I continue to report to my functional Manager while I am in the project
186	Resources	Beneficiary	People	How will my performance appraisal be done?
187	Resources	Beneficiary	People	How much time am I assigned to the project?
188	Resources	Beneficiary	People	Are other team members who can complement my skills?
189	Resources	Beneficiary	People	Is there a vacation freeze in the project?
190	Resources	Beneficiary	People	Is the project plan resource leveled?

191	Resources	Initiator	Software	What are the licensing fees for the software tools to be used?
192	Resources	Initiator	Software	How can freeware tools be leveraged in the project?
193	Resources	Implementer	Software	How to prevent the users from uploading dangerous files? (php, cgi, exe, et cetera)
194	Resources	Implementer	Software	What are the commercial tools used in the project?
195	Resources	Beneficiary	Software	Does every piece of input that comes from an untrusted source (i.e. the user, or other systems) gets filtered?
196	Resources	Initiator	Hardware	What is the cost of hardware (PC, Printers, Servers, and Routers et cetera) to be used?
197	Resources	Beneficiary	Hardware	Is the hardware reliable?
198	Resources	Initiator	Communication Facilities	What is the cost of Telephone, Fax and internet?
199	Resources	Implementer	Communication Facilities	Are the communication facilities reliable?
200	Resources	Beneficiary	Communication Facilities	How do I communicate to the project team?
201	Resources	Initiator	Facilities	What is the seat costs?
202	Resources	Initiator	Facilities	What is the risk of remote delivery?
203	Resources	Implementer	Facilities	Are the ergonomics considered in the facilities?
204	Resources	Beneficiary	Facilities	Are the teams co-located?

Appendix 2

The Eight Measures in the Measurement Model

Size/Scope Measures

Quantifying size is one of the most basic and critical activities in software measurement. Size/scope is the work that needs to be accomplished to deliver a product or service with the specified features and functions. Though there are many measures for size the two size measures that are most suited for a software project are.

1. Physical size (i.e. Lines of code).

   Physical size is basically the size of the source code of software. Its key features are:

   • Describes the system itself.
   • Represents the size from the development perspective.
   • Easier to define objectively.

2. Functional size (i.e. Function points).

   Functional Size is the software size in terms of the output delivered to the user - the software functionality. Its key features are:

   • Describes the business functionality provided by the system.

- Represents the functionality from the end user's perspective.
- It is subjective.

Lines of Code (LOC)

The Lines of code (LOC) measure was formally proposed by Wolverton to formally measure programmer productivity [Wolverton, 1974]. The most common definition of LOC is to count any programming statement without the blank or comment line. It is mainly the count of instruction statements. According to SEI, the LOC is the most widely used metric for program size [Mills, 1988] and Fenton also concurs with this finding [Fenton, 2006]. LOC is very important in the testing phases of the project and maintenance of the product after the project completion particularly for support effort estimation. In addition, LOC is an effective tool for understanding other metrics. Almost any code or testing metric that suffers a sharp spike or sudden drop requires a look at total LOC for more analysis.

There are two major types of LOC measures: Physical LOC (LOC) and Logical LOC (LLOC). Physical LOC is a count of lines in the text of the program's source code including comment lines. Logical LOC measures the number of "statements", but their definitions are tied to specific computer languages. For example, logical LOC in C programming language is the number of key word terminating statements. Consider this snippet of C code as an example of the two types of LOC.

For (i = 0; i < 100; i += 1) printf ("Hello World"); /* LOC Determination*/
In this example there are:
1 Physical Lines of Code (LOC)
2 Logical Line of Code (LOC) (for statement and printf statement)
1 comment line

Depending on the programmer and/or coding standards, the above program could be even written on many separate lines as shown below.

For (i = 0; i < 100; i += 1)

```
{
    printf("Hello World");
}
```

In this example there are:

5 Physical Lines of Code (LOC)

2 Logical Line of Code (LLOC)

1 comment line

The second example is much easier to read and debug during maintenance than the earlier "spaghetti" code. In addition, it is found to be much easier to create tools that measure physical LOC, and physical LOC definitions are easier to explain. So physical LOC will be used as the definition for LOC. Although LOC can be useful as it is an easy, fast and inexpensive method to estimate size, it has two important drawbacks.

The number of LOC is dependent on the implementation language and coding style of the programmers. For instance, 10,000 LOC in C programming language can be reduced by a couple of hundreds or less LOC in Java, as Java gives many libraries to wrap common programming instructions.(Libraries contain code and data to provide services in a modular fashion to independent programs). Also experienced programmers use less variables and LOC in a program than inexperienced programmers.

LOC cannot be determined before coding. Only when coding for the functionality is completed it is possible to count the number of lines in a software product and hence determine the size. Hence the estimate of the size (and subsequent related activities such as effort estimation) cannot be carried out before the development is complete.

Function Points (FPs)

LOC is a technical measure and it does not measure the size of the business functions covered in the project deliverables. In addition, LOC is only known when the development is done. However in many project situations such as effort estimation we have to know the size of the component for scheduling development tasks, budgeting et cetera. In this situation, functional size measurement is needed as it is aimed at measuring the size of the software product from the perspective of what gets delivered to the end user in terms of business functionality. Functional size measurement is considered the ultimate measure of software productivity as it provides the number of functions regardless of the software [Kan, 2003].

There are two primary functional sizing methodologies: Function Point Analysis and COSMIC-FFP and the Function Point Analysis method proposed by defined by Allan Albrecht is the recommended option [Symons, 2001]. FPs provides the measure of software size that can be determined early in the development process and can be very helpful in size/effort estimation. The size reported in terms of FPs is independent of the computer language, development methodology, technology or capability of the project team used to develop the application. A typical function point analysis consists of the following four steps:

Step 1: Determine the type of function point count (users, purpose, and dependencies)

Based on the design specifications, the following system functions are measured i.e. counted.

- Inputs
- Outputs
- Files
- Inquires
- Interfaces

The three components i.e. External Inputs (EI), External Outputs (EO) and External Inquiries (EQ) add, modify, delete, retrieve or processes information contained in the files and hence are called transactions. The other two components are the system's files viz., Internal Logical Files (ILF) and External Interface Files (EIF) and these are called data functions.

Step 2: Calculate the Unadjusted Function Point (UFP)

These function-point counts are then weighed (multiplied) by their degree of complexity. This is reflected in table A based on historical data from real world projects [IFPUG, 1999].

Table A: Function Point Factors

	Simple	Average	Complex
Inputs	3	4	6
Outputs	4	5	7
Files	7	10	15
Inquires	3	4	6
Interfaces	5	7	10

For example, if an application has nine external inputs which are all simple, eight external outputs which are of average complexity, fourteen simple internal files, seven simple external inquiries and fifteen high complexity interfaces the unadjusted Function Count (FC) = 3*9 +5* 8 + 14*7+ 7*3 +15*10 = 336

Step 3: Determine the Value Adjustment Factor (VAF) to account for factors that affect the project and/or system as a whole.

There will be a number of technical and operational factors a.k.a non-functional requirements (NFR) such as performance, reusability, usability et cetera that affect the size of the project. From the FP calculation perspective, there are 14 'General System Characteristics", or GSCs, and each one is ranked from "0" for no influence to "5" for essential to account for the complexity of the software system. The ranking for all these factors are added, to get a Value Adjustment factor (VAF) for the measurement object. When the values of these 14 GSCs were summed up we get the "Total Degree of Influence", or TDI value.

$VAF = 0.65 + (TDI*0.01)$

So the VAF can vary in range from 0.65 (when all GSCs are low i.e. GSC = 0) to 1.35 (when all GSCs are high i.e. GSC = 14*5 = 70). Let us assume, all the values from the fourteen factors add up to 44. So the Value Adjustment Factor (VAF) = 0.65 + 0.01*44 = 1.09

Step 4: Calculate the adjusted function point (FP) count

So the adjusted FP = FC * VAF = 336 * 1.09 = 366. This figure is the quantifiable metric on the size of the functional scope/size.

Function points have their own advantages and disadvantages. The advantages are:

- Uses language meaningful to non-programmers including end users.
- Measures system primarily from logical perspective independent of the implementation technology.
- Normalizes data across various projects and organizations.
- Can be used as a reference for estimating key project parameters

The disadvantages with Function points are:

- It is a labor-intensive method and expensive for applications greater than 15,000 FPs.
- It requires significant training and experience to be proficient for FP counting.
- It is subjective to some extent as the functional complexity weights and degrees of influence are determined by trial and error. Though there is lot of historical data to be leveraged to reduce the variation, FPs still bring some amount to subjectivity.

Complexity Measure

The McCabe cyclomatic complexity v (G) and Halstead's software science (HSS) are two common code or product complexity measures. However McCabe cyclomatic complexity v (G) is more popular from the implementation perspective in the industry [Fenton, 2006]. In addition (G) is available in most commercial development editors.

To measure the technical i.e. the structural complexity of a program, Thomas J. McCabe developed a measure called the McCabe cyclomatic complexity (v (G)). This measure counts the available decision paths in the program thereby placing a numerical value on the complexity [McCabe, 1979]. This brings practicability and simplicity to the software development process as programmers know that module with many IF/THEN statements is hard to debug and understand. In addition, empirical data has provided a high correlation between defect rates and cyclomatic complexity in the programs.

The McCabe complexity has its roots in graph theory. If G is the control flow graph of program P and G has e edges (arcs) and n nodes, then $v (G) (P) = e-n+2$ where v (G) (P) is the number of linearly independent paths in G. In the below figure, e = 16 n =13. This gives v (G) (P) = 5. More simply, if d is the number of decision nodes in G then $v (G) (P) = d+1$. In the below figure 4.3, d = 4. Incidentally McCabe proposed v (G) (P) < 10 for each program module P.

For instance, the following simple Java method for the below decision model shown in figure A will yield a McCabe's cyclomatic complexity value of 3.

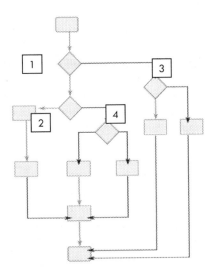

Figure A: McCabe Complexity Example

```
public int getValue(int param1) {
    int value = 0;
    if (param1 == 0)
        {value = 4;}
    else
        {value = 0;}    }
    return value;
}
```

In the method above, there are two decision points: an if and an else; and the method's entry point automatically adds one taking the final value to 3. The more control statements such as "if", "while", "for" et cetera in the code the higher the McCabe's cyclomatic complexity of the code. Based on the computed value, the below table B from the SEI, categorizes the program based on the complexity at class or file level [SEI, 1997].

Table B: Original McCabe values for Program complexity

Cyclomatic Complexity	Code Complexity
1-10	A simple program, without much risk
11-20	Medium complex, moderate risk
21-50	Complex, high risk
51+	Un-testable, very high risk

So in the above example, the program constructed is a "simple program, without much risk" as the McCabe cyclomatic complexity value of 3.

The main advantages of McCabe Cyclomatic Complexity are:

- It is intuitive and easy to apply.
- It can be computed relatively early in lifecycle.
- Development editors such as Visual Studio integrated development environment (IDE), Eclipse, IntelliJ et cetera already have McCabe's cyclomatic complexity as part of their metric suite for application lifecycle management.

Some of the drawbacks of McCabe Cyclomatic Complexity are:

- It is only a measure of the program's technical complexity and not the data complexity associated with the program.
- Same weight is placed on nested and non-nested loops. Although the number of control paths relates to code complexity, this number is only part of the complexity picture.
- McCabe's Cyclomatic Complexity is a summary index of binary decisions. It does not distinguish different kinds of control flow complexity such as loops versus IF-THEN-ELSES or cases versus IF-THEN-ELSES.

Earned Value Management (EVM) to measure Project Schedule and Cost

Earned value management (EVM) is a project management technique for measuring project progress in an objective manner by combining measurements of scope, schedule, and cost in a single integrated system. It is a systematic project management process used to find variances in projects based on the comparison of work performed and work planned leveraging the fundamental principle that pattern and trends of the past can be good predictors of the future. According to the Project Management Institute (PMI), EVM is the most effective project measurement tool where schedule and cost can be measured objectively by comparing the amount of work that was planned with what was actually accomplished [PMI, 2008].

The key component of EVM is the project baseline a.k.a. Performance Measurement Baseline (PMB). The PMB is the time-phased budget plan for accomplishing work, against which project performance is measured as per stakeholder needs. For management, it provides the ability to review the "original" i.e. baselined projected spending over time and predict a completion date and cost based on a projection of trends experienced to date on the project. For project managers, it provides a tool to review the cost and schedule variance. For team members, it affords an objective perspective on their targets over time.

Building Blocks of EVM

There are three basic elements of EVM which is normally expressed in monetary units such as Dollars, Euros et cetera. The figure B below provides an overview of these elements [Wilkens, 1999].

1. Planned Value (PV).

PV is the total cost of the work scheduled/planned as of a reporting date. It is recorded when the work is planned showing the cumulative resources budgeted across the project schedule [PMI, 2004].

2. Actual Cost (AC)

AC is the total cost taken to complete the work as of a reporting date. AC is the indication of the level of resources expended to achieve the actual work performed to date [PMI, 2004].This can be calculated as Hourly Rate * Total Hours Spent.

3. Earned Value (EV).

EV is the total cost of the work completed as of a reporting date [PMI, 2004]. For instance, EV is calculated as Planned Value * % Complete Actual.

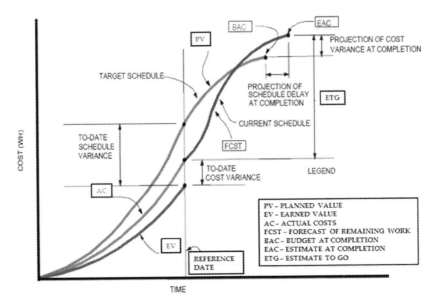

Figure B: Building blocks of EVM

Using these three numbers i.e. PV, EV and AC, the schedule (SPI) and the cost measures (CPI) are derived.

Implementing EVM

The success of EVM is dependent on the rigorous use of project management tools and processes such as planning, controlling, reporting, forecasting et cetera. In addition, implementation of EVM demands tailoring of the time/effort reporting and accounting system to allow time and cost to be tracked to specific WBS elements in the project. Following are the four key steps involved in the implementation.

Step 1: Build the Work Breakdown Structure (WBS).

Identifying the scope is the first step in project management and EVM is no exception to this. Once the scope is identified, it must be decomposed at manageable levels into the Work breakdown Structure (WBS). In the WBS the project is decomposed into elements and each element successively decomposed into component elements until the hierarchy of the complete scope of work is developed.

Step 2: Schedule the activities, allocate efforts/costs and baseline the plan.

Some projects follow the start-up sequence of scope, schedule, and budget while others follow scope, budget, and schedule. But the outcome at the end of this step is to schedule the activities (after the effort is estimated) with the allocated costs to each Control account in the WBS. This plan should be baselined to form the PMB after the project plan is verified and approved by all project stakeholders.

Step 3: Update project progress regularly to derive EV.

Once the project work is underway, the project plan should be updated regularly on the work accomplished with appropriate earning rules as the percentage of the work accomplished to get the earned value (EV). Also actual costs associated with each activity should be simultaneously maintained for each CA and this information can come from time sheets and invoices to the project.

Step 4: Perform calculations, analyze the reports and take corrective actions

To measure schedule, EVM uses a Schedule Performance Index (SPI) which is an index showing the efficiency of the time utilized on the project. SPI can be calculated using the following formula:

SPI = Earned Value (EV) /Planned Value (PV)

Closely associated with SPI is the schedule variance (SV) which indicates how much ahead or behind schedule the project is.

SV = Earned Value (EV) - Planned Value (PV)

To measure cost, EVM uses Cost Performance Index (CPI). According to Fleming and Koppelman, the CPI is likely the single most important metric for any project employing earned value [Fleming and Koppelman, 2000]. CPI is an index showing the efficiency of the utilization of the resources on the project and can be calculated using the following formula:

CPI = Earned Value (EV) /Actual Cost (AC)

Cost Variance (CV) is closely associated with CPI and it indicates how much over or under budget the project is.

Cost Variance (CV) = Earned Value (EV) - Actual Cost (AC)

Table C below shows how the EVM performance measures indicate the project status with respect to the schedule and budget.

Table C: Interpretations of Basic EVM
Performance Measures [PMI, 2004]

Performance Measures		SV & SPI		
		>0 & >1.0	=0 & = 1.0	<0 & <1.0
CV & CPI	>0 & >1.0	Ahead of Schedule & Under Budget	On Schedule & Under Budget	Behind Schedule & Under Budget
	=0 & = 1.0	Ahead of Schedule & On Budget	On Schedule & On Budget	Behind Schedule & On Budget
	<0 & <1.0	Ahead of Schedule & Over Budget	On Schedule & Over Budget	Behind Schedule & Over Budget

EVM serves to illustrate the difference between what was planned and what is actually happening against the PMB. It is an early warning system that alerts management to the realities of project performance promoting the philosophy of management by exception.

Quality Measures

According to Phil Crosby, "Quality is conformance to requirements; both functional and non-functional requirements" [Crossby, 1995]. So when the requirements are met, quality is achieved; and any nonconformance to the requirement is reported as a defect. So quality can be improved in the project by identifying and resolving the defects. In this backdrop, three measures associated with defects were identified.

1. Sigma Level (Cpk). This gives an indicator of the effectiveness and stability of the software development process in the project.
2. Defect Density (DD). This reflects the complexity and stability of different components in the project.
3. Defects Removal Efficiency (DRE).This provides information on the rate at which defects are resolved.

Sigma Level (Cpk)

Process stability is considered as the core of process management where the process is defined as unique combination of tools, materials, methods, and people engaged in producing a measurable output. When a process is stable and conforming to requirements, it is termed capable. The Process capability is the capability of a process to meet its intended purpose i.e. the ability of a process to produce output within specification limits. When a process is under statistical control, the variation is within predictable limits. A good capable process i.e. the voice of the process (VOP) is one where almost all the measurements fall inside the specification limits which would be the voice of the customer(VOC). Process capability depends on both the stability of the process (VOP) and its ability to conform to customer requirements (VOC). Thus a capable process is a stable process whose performance satisfies customer requirements.

Process Capability Index (Cpk) for calculating the sigma level uses Defects per million opportunities (DPMO) to indicate the effectiveness of the SDLC process; higher sigma level indicates that the process is less likely to create defects.

$$DPMO = \frac{Total\ Number\ of\ Defects}{Total\ Opportunity\ (TO)} \times 1,000,000$$

In the DPMO equation, Total Opportunities (TO) is the count of number of defects that can be identified. The number of opportunities is normally proportional to the size (LOC/FPs). The sigma level and the corresponding DPMO is as shown in the table D below.

Table D: Sigma Level V/s DPMO

Sigma Level	DPMO (with 1.5 Sigma shift)
1.5	500,000
3.0	66,800
4.0	6,210
5.0	230
6.0	3.4

For example, in a software project potentially every test case is an opportunity for a defect. If there are 106 test cases/opportunities and 7 defects reported during testing. This is equivalent to 66,037 DPMO (= 7/106 * 1,000,000) or 3 sigma.

Defect Density (DD)

Defect density (DD) is among the most important measures of software reliability as it gives an objective way of comparing different functionalities in the project. It is a measure of the total known defects divided by the size of the software entity being measured. Lower the DD, better it is. According to Steve McConnell, one of the easiest ways to judge whether a program is ready for release is to measure its defect density [McConnell, 1997]. The formula for Defect density is given by:

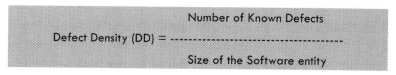

The "Number of known defects" i.e. the numerator is the count of total defects identified against a particular software entity, in a particular time period in a software project. Size is a normalizer that allows comparisons between different software entities (i.e. modules, releases, products) and is counted either in LOC or FPs. Capers Jones strongly recommends not using LOC as a basis for metrics like DD as they are known to vary by a factor of 10 when compared with FPs. He recommends looking at DD in light of FPs given that FP is invariant with solution size [Jones, 1996]. Hence FPs is considered as the measure for size while calculating DD.

For example, if there are eight defects reported during testing for one function "X" that has nine function points, then the defect density is 8/9 which is 0.9. However a second function "Y" with seven function points might have four defects giving a defect density of 4/7 which is 0.55. So if one has to compare the two functions, function Y is more stable than function X. This information will be particularly helpful as DD serves as a comparator between different modules so that the project team can focus on few critical modules. Also the DD measure can be used to perform a release or iteration wise comparison of quality efforts to see if the quality initiatives implemented are being realized.

Defect Removal Efficiency (DRE)

Defect removal is one of the top expenses in any software project and it greatly affects project schedules. Capers Jones says, "Defect-removal efficiency (DRE) is a simple and powerful software quality metric that should be understood by everyone in the software business as it can provide very sophisticated analysis and change "quality" from an ambiguous, amorphous term to a tangible factor [Jones, 1996]".DRE can be of 2 types:

1. DRE across the SDLC
2. DRE in a particular phase.

1. Defect Removal Efficiency (DRE) across the SDLC

This calculation is complex as it includes the latency aspect in defects. In this case the Defect Removal Efficiency (DRE) is calculated as:

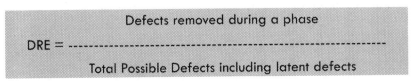

$$DRE = \frac{\text{Defects removed during a phase}}{\text{Total Possible Defects including latent defects}}$$

According to Capers Jones's rule of thumb [Jones, 1996], Function points raised to the power of 1.25 predicts the approximate total number of defects in a new software project. Though ideal value of DRE should be 1, world class organizations have DRE greater than 95% and apply approximately the following sequence of at least eight defect removal activities to reach that level of DRE effectiveness [Jones, 1995].

- Design inspections
- Code inspections
- Unit test
- New function test
- Regression test
- Performance test
- System test
- External Beta test

Also defect prediction studies are done on LOC and v (G) metrics using regression based "data fitting" models which provide reasonable estimates for the total number of defects D which is actually defined as the sum of the defects found during testing and the defects found during two months after release. Gaffney provided the programming language independent relationship between D and LOC (Lines of Code) using the following polynomial equation [Gaffney, 1984; Fenton, 1999]. The LOC in turn is tied to v (G).

$$D = 4.2 + 0.0015(LOC)^{4/3}$$

So the denominator in the DRE i.e. "Total Possible Defects including latent defects" is Maximum (Capers' Rule of Thumb, Gaffney's Equation). The maximum of the two results is taken so that the DRE value is on a conservative side. For instance, if a software project has 100 function points, the maximum number of potential defects i.e. D as per Capers' rule of thumb will be POW (100, 1.25) which will be 316. For the same project if 12500 LOC are written, then D according to Gaffney's Equation will be 439 defects. So the "Total Possible Defects including latent defects" = Maximum (316,439) = 439. The table E below gives the statistics for project teams on the DRE based on their software engineering process maturity [Longstreet, 2008].

Table E: DRE v/s Process Maturity

Activity	High Maturity	Medium Maturity	Poor Maturity
Requirements Reviews	15%	5%	0%
Design Reviews	30%	15%	0%
Code Reviews	20%	10%	0%
Formal Testing	25%	15%	15%
Total Percentage Removed	90%	45%	15%

So if a project team is at a high level of software engineering maturity, there will be still 10% of the defects not fixed at the end of the testing phase that will be "latent" for the next phase. In the above example, the project would still have up to 44 defects (10%) after all defect discovery and resolution efforts.

2. Defect Removal Efficiency (DRE) in a particular phase

In this case, DRE is calculated as a ratio of defects resolved to total number of defects found. For example, suppose that 100 defects were found during the testing stage and 84 defects were resolved by the development team at the moment of measurement. The DRE would be calculated as 84 divided by 100 which is 84%.

DRE across the SDLC i.e. option # 1 is recommended as it gives a holistic status of the project across the SDLC.

Appendix 3

Definition of the 14 Validation Criteria

1. **Appropriate Continuity**

   A metric has appropriate continuity if the metric is defined for all values according to the attribute being measured [Kitchenham et al, 1995].

2. **Appropriate Granularity.**

   A metric has **appropriate granularity** if the mapping from attribute to metric is not too finely- or coarsely-grained [Kitchenham et al, 1995]. Granularity (or the measurement increment) refers to how divisible the value of the measurement unit or measure is. Too fine a granularity may also make it difficult to provide business value and too coarse a granularity increases complexity and decreases readability. Granularity can be fine, medium, and coarse granularity.

   - A metric has **fine granularity** if there are only finitely many programs that can achieve a given measure. For example, the cyclomatic number is not finely grained as one can create an infinite number of programs that have the same cyclomatic number.
   - A metric has **medium granularity** if there are two programs that compute the same function, but have different measures. This property is based on the idea that

different programs can perform identical functionality with differing implementations and, therefore, result in different complexities. For example, cyclomatic complexity has medium granularity because one can write two programs that have different complexities, but still perform the same functionality.

- A metric has **coarse granularity** if two different programs can result in the same measure. That is, not every measurement needs to be unique to a specific program. The two programs can represent two different implementations altogether (not just renamings of each other) and can still have the same complexity value.

3. Association

A metric has **association validity** if it has a direct, linear statistical correlation with an external quality factor [Schneidewind 1991], [Fenton, 1994]. Measurement of this criterion is typically done by the correlation coefficient.

4. Attribute validity

A metric has **attribute validity** if the measurements correctly exhibit the attribute that the metric is intending to measure [Kitchenham et al. 1995].

5. Discriminative Power

A metric has **discriminative power** if it can show a difference between high-quality and low-quality components by examining components above/below a pre-determined critical value [Schneidewind 1991].

6. Dimensional Consistency

A metric has **dimensional consistency** if the formulation of multiple metrics into a composite metric is performed by a scientifically well-understood mathematical function [Kitchenham et al, 1995].

7. Instrument validity

A metric has **instrument validity** if the underlying measurement instrument is valid and properly calibrated [Kitchenham et al, 1995].

8. Predictability

A metric has **predictability** if it can be shown to predict values of an external quality factor with an acceptable level of accuracy [Fenton 1994],[Schneidewind 1991], [El Emam 2000].

9. Protocol validity

Protocol validity is whether an acceptable measurement protocol is adopted. Fundamentally protocol validity of measurement entity is a function of attribute, scales and dimension analysis.

10. Repeatability

A metric has repeatability if the metric is shown to be empirically valid for multiple different projects or throughout the lifetime of one projects [Schneidewind 1991], [El Emam, 2000].

11. Representation Condition:

A measure essentially maps real world attributes to a numerical domain i.e. to a set of integers, rational numbers, or real numbers. In other words, our observations in the real world must be reflected in the numerical values we obtain from the mathematical world. If we call this mapping f, then the measured value of object/entity x is f(x) i.e. "f" is the mapping between real world domain and the numerical domain. This mapping is called representation or homomorphism, because the measure represents the attribute in the numerical world and is illustrated in figure C below.

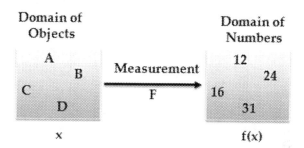

Figure C: Measurement Mapping.

12. Scale validity

Scales yield numbers that represent properties of the objects they measure. A measure has **scale validity** if it is defined on an explicit, appropriate scale such that all meaningful transformations of the metric are admissible [Briand et al, 1995], [El Emam 2000].

13. Trackability

A metric has **trackability** if the metric changes as the external quality factor changes over time [Schneidewind 1991].

14. Unit validity

A measure has **unit validity** if the measures used are an appropriate means of measuring the attribute. Although unit definition models may be influenced by a desire to measure a specific attribute of a specific entity type, they usually include some concept of the attribute that is affected by the scale. A measure can be categorized as belonging to one of the four types of unit definition models:

1. **Standard Definition.**
   Here measures are selected in reference to a standard definition. For example, LOC is defined as a non-blank, non-comment physical line in the program.

2. **Theoretical Model.**
   This includes referring to the wider accepted theory and involves the way in which an attribute is observed on a particular entity. For example, an "executable statement" can be defined by reference to the manner in which a compiler handles particular elements of a specific programming language.

3. **Conversion Model.**
   Here the measures are derived from conversion from another measure. For example, "system size" is defined as the sum of its module sizes. This type of definition is controlled by the scale type of the units as the scale type determines the appropriate mappings from one unit to another.

4. **Composite Model.**
   This model is constructed involving several attributes. For example, the unit "hours per line of code" can be used to measure productivity because we define productivity to be the effort to produce a given amount of software.

Appendix 4

Survey Questionnaire

The participants were requested to rate the eight measures in the below set of nine questions on a scale of 0 to 5 as follows.

0 - Never heard of this Measure.

1 – Strongly Disagree

2 – Disagree

3 – Neither Agree nor Disagree

4 – Agree

5 – Strongly Agree

The nine questions are:

1. Can **Function Points (FPs)** measure the size of the software project objectively before development?

2. Can **Lines of Code (LOC)** measure the size of the software project objectively after development?

3. Can **McCabe's Cyclomatic Complexity (VG)** measure the complexity of the software project objectively for software maintenance?

4. Can **Cost Performance Index (CPI)** measure/track the cost/effort of the software project objectively?

5. Can **Schedule Performance Index (SPI)** measure/track the schedule of the software project objectively?

6. Can **Sigma level (Cpk)** measure/track the quality of the software development process in the project objectively?

7. Can **Defect Density (DD)** measure/track the quality of one software component against another in the project?

8. Can **Defect Removal Efficiency (DRE)** measure/track the efficiency of defects resolved in the project?

9. Can these **8 Core measures in totality (OM)** describe the accurate and objective status of the software project (within +/- 10% of the schedule and cost for the base-lined scope)?

References

- Albert, Cecilia and Brownsword, Lisa, 2002, "Evolutionary Process for Integrating COTS-Based Systems (EPIC): An Overview", TECHNICAL REPORT CMU/SEI-2002-TR-009 ESC-TR-2002-009.
- Basili, Victor R, Gianluigi Caldiera, and Rombach, H. Dieter, 1994, "The Goal Question Metric Approach", Encyclopedia of Software Engineering, Wiley.
- Basili, Victor, Shull, Forrest and Lanubile, Filippo, 1999, "Using Experiments to Build a Body of Knowledge", PSI '99 Proceedings of the Third International Andrei Ershov Memorial Conference on Perspectives of System Informatics.
- 2007, "Bridging the gap between business strategy and software development", 28th International Conference on Information Systems, Montreal, Canada.
- Berander, Patrik and Per, Jönsson, September 21–22, 2006. "A Goal Question Metric Based Approach for Efficient Measurement Framework Definition", ISESE'06, Rio de Janeiro, Brazil.
- Briand, Lionel, El Emam, Khaled and Morasca, Sandro, 1995, "Theoretical and Empirical Validation of Software Product Measures", International Software Engineering Research Network.
- Briand, Lionel, El Emam, Khaled and Morasca, Sandro, 1996, "On the Application of Measurement Theory in Software Engineering", International Software Engineering Research Network (ISERN).
- Brooks, Frederick, 1995, "The Mythical Man-Month", 20th Edition, Pearson Education.
- Card, D.N and Jones, C.L, November 2003, "Status report: Practical Software Measurement", Proceedings of the third International Conference on Quality Software, pp 315-320.

- Chen, W and Hirschheim, R, 2004, "A paradigmatic and methodological examination of information systems research from 1991 to 2001", Information Systems Journal, 14 (3), 197-235.
- Chen, Kung H and Shimerda, Thomas A, Spring 1981, "An Empirical Analysis of Useful Financial Ratios", Financial Management, Vol. 10, No. 1, pp. 51-60
- Creswell, J. W. (2005). Educational research: Planning, conducting, and evaluating quantitative and qualitative research (2nd ed.). Upper Saddle River, NJ: Pearson.
- Crosby, Philip B, 1995, "Quality Without Tears: The Art of Hassle-Free Management", pp. 59, McGraw-Hill Professional.
- Curtis, Bill and Jones, Capers, 2009, CISQ 2009 Executive Forums Report.
- Dalcher Darren, October 2009, "Software Project Success: Moving Beyond Failure", The European Journal of Informatics Professional, Volume 10, Issue 5.
- Dekkers, Carol and McQuaid, Patricia, Mar/Apr 2000, "The Dangers of Using Software Metrics to (Mis) Manage", IT Professional, vol. 4 no. 2, pp. 24-30.
- DeLone, W. H., and McLean, E. R, Spring 2003, "The DeLone and McLean Model of Information Systems Success: A Ten-Year Update", Journal of Management Information Systems (19:4), pp. 9-30.
- Downing, Steven M, "Validity: on the meaningful interpretation of assessment data", Medical Education, Volume 37, Issue 9, pages 830–837, September 2003.
- Dowling, Ted, 2000, "Software COTS Components – Problems, And Solutions?", RTO SCI Symposium on "Strategies to Mitigate Obsolescence in Defense Systems Using Commercial Components", held in Budapest, Hungary, 23-25 October 2000.
- El Emam, K, June 2000, "A Methodology for Validating Software Product Metrics", National Research Council of Canada, NCR-ERC-1076.
- Ellis, T. J., & Levy, Y. (2008). A framework of problem-based research: A guide for novice researchers on the development of a research-worthy problem. Informing Science: The International Journal of an Emerging Transdiscipline, 11, 17-33

- Fairley, R.E. 2009. Managing and Leading Software Projects. Hoboken, NJ, USA: John Wiley and Sons.
- Fenton, E Norman and Pfleeger, SL, 1997, "Software Metrics: A Rigorous and Practical Approach", PWS Publishing Company.
- Fenton, E Norman and Neil, Martin, 1999, "Software metrics: successes, failures, and new directions", Journal of Systems and Software.
- Fenton, E Norman, September/October 1999, "A Critique of Software Defect Prediction Models", IEEE transactions on Software Engineering, Volume 25, Number 6.
- Fenton, E Norman, September 2006, "New Directions for Software Metrics", CIO Symposium on Software Best Practices.
- Fleming, Quentin W and Koppelman, Joel M, July 1998. "Earned Value Management – A Powerful Tool for Software Projects", Journal of Defense Software Engineering.
- Fleming, Quentin W and Koppelman, Joel M, 2000, "Earned Value Project Management, Second Edition", PM World Today, Volume 8, Issue 8.
- Fleming, Quentin W and Koppelman, Joel M, 2006, "Start with simple Earned Value on all your projects", Project Management Institute.
- Frappier, M., Matwin, S., Mili, A, 1994, "Software Metrics for Predicting Maintainability. Software Metrics Study", Tech. Memo. 2. Canadian Space Agency.
- Gable, GG, 1994, "Integrating case study and survey research methods: an example in information systems ", European Journal of Information Systems, Volume 3, No 2, pp 112-126.
- Gray, Martha M, November-December 1999, "Applicability of Metrology to Information Technology", Journal of Research of the National Institute of Standards and Technology, Volume 104, Number 6.
- Gross, Joshua B, April 2006, "End User Software Engineering: Auditing the Invisible", WEUSE II Workshop, Montréal, Quebec, Canada.
- Guba, E.G, 1990,"The Paradigm Dialog", Sage Publications
- Hevner, A. R, March, T. S, Park, J and Sudha, R, 2004, "Design Science in Information Systems Research", MIS Quarterly, 28 (1), 75-105.
- Humphrey, Watts, 1999, "Managing the Software Process", Pearson Education.

- Humphrey Watts S, March 2005, "Why Big Software Projects Fail: The 12 key Questions", Journal of Defense Software Engineering.
- ISO/IEC 15939, 2007, "Systems and software engineering -Measurement process"
- Jackson, Peter, "Getting Design Right: A Systems Approach", CRC Press; 1 edition, 2009
- Johnson, Burke and Christensen, Larry, "Educational research: quantitative, qualitative, and mixed approaches", Sage Publications, 2004
- Jones, Capers, 2002, "Software Estimating Rules of Thumb", IEEE Software, vol. 29, no. 3, pp. 116.
- Jones, Capers, 2008, "Applied Software Measurement: Global Analysis of Productivity and Quality", 3rd Edition, McGraw-Hill Osborne Media
- Kan, Stephen, 2003, "Metrics and Models in Software Quality Engineering", 2nd Edition, Pearson Education.
- Kaner, Cem and Bond, Walter P, 2004, "Software Engineering Metrics: What Do They Measure and How Do We Know", 10th International Software Metrics Symposium.
- Kaplan, R S and Norton, D P, Jan – Feb 1992, "The balanced scorecard: measures that drive performance", Harvard Business Review, pp. 71–80.
- Kerzner, Harold, 2003, "Project Management: A Systems Approach to Planning, Scheduling, and Controlling", 8th Edition, Wiley.
- Kitchenham, Barbara, Pfleeger, SL and Fenton, Norman, December 1995, "Towards a Framework for Software Measurement Validation", IEEE Transactions on Software Engineering, Volume 21 Issue 12.
- Leedy, P. D., & Ormrod, J. E., 2005, "Practical research: Planning and design", Upper Saddle River, NJ: Prentice Hall.
- Longstreet, David, 2008, "Reboot! Rethinking and Restarting Software Development".
- Lukas, Joseph, 2008, "Earned Value Analysis – Why it doesn't work", AACE International Transactions
- McConnell, Steve, 2006, "Software Estimation: Demystifying the Black Art", Microsoft Press.
- McConnell, Steve, May/June 1997, "Gauging Software Readiness with Defect Tracking", IEEE Software, Vol. 14, No. 3.

- McGarry, John, Card, David, Jones, Cheryl, Beth Layman, Clark, Elizabeth, Dean, Joseph Dean, Hall, Fred, 2001, "Practical software measurement: objective information for decision makers", Addison-Wesley Professional.
- McGrath, J. 1982, "Dilemmatics: The study of research choices and dilemmas", Judgment calls in research: 69-80. Sage Publications, USA.
- Meneely Andrew, Smith Ben, Williams, Laurie, 2010, "Software Metrics Validation Criteria – A Systematic Literature review", Transactions on Software Engineering Methodologies.
- Mills, Everald, 1988, "Software Metrics", SEI Curriculum Module SEI-CM-12-1.1, Carnegie Melon Software Engineering Institute.
- Moller KH and Paulish DJ, 1993, "Software metrics: A practitioner's guide to improved product development", 1st Edition, IEEE Computer Society Press
- Niehaves, Bjorn, "Epistemological Perspectives on Multi-Method Information Systems Research" (2005). ECIS 2005 Proceedings. Paper 120
- Pfleeger SL, Ross Jeffery, Bill Curtis, Barbara Kitchenham, 2002, "Status Report on Software Measurement", IEEE Software, Volume 14, Issue 2, pp 33-43.
- Pfleeger, SL, Nov /Dec. 2008, "Software Metrics: Progress after 25 Years?", IEEE Software, vol. 25, no. 6, pp. 32-34.
- PMI, 2008, "PMBOK 4th Edition", Project Management Institute.
- Pressman, Roger, 2004, "Software Engineering: A Practitioner's Approach", 6th Edition, McGraw-Hill publications.
- Putnam, Larry and Meyers, Ware, August 2002, "Control the Software Beast With Metrics-Based Management", The Journal of Defense Software Engineering.
- QSM, November 2009, "Function Point Languages Table- Version 4.0". http://www.qsm.com/?q=resources/function-point-languages-table/index.html
- Rad, Parviz F and Levin, Ginger, September 2005, "Metrics for Project Management: Formalized Approaches", Management Concepts; 1 edition.
- Reel, John S, May/June 1999, "Critical Success Factors in Software Projects", IEEE Software, Volume 16 Issue 3.
- Reichheld, Frederick, December 2003, "The One Number You Need to Grow", Harvard Business Review.

- Schneidewind, Norman F, May 1992, "Methodology for Validating Software Metrics", IEEE Transactions on Software Engineering, Volume 18, Number 5.
- Sirvio, Komi, 2003, "Development and Evaluation of Software Process Improvement Methods – Doctoral Dissertation", VTT Publications.
- Smith, Larry, December 2000, "Project Clarity Through Stakeholder Analysis", CROSSTALK The Journal of Defense Software Engineering.
- Soni Devpriya, Shrivastava Ritu and Kumar M, 2009, "A Framework for Validation of Object Oriented Design Metrics", International Journal of Computer Science and Information Security, Vol. 6, No.3.
- Stake, Robert, 1995, "The Art of case study Research", Thousand Oaks Publications.
- Standish Group, 2009, "Chaos Summary 2009 Report".
- Thomas, Graeme and Fernandez, Walter, "Success in IT projects: A matter of definition?", International Journal of Project Management, Volume 26, Issue 7, October 2008, Pages 733-742
- Trochim, William and Donnelly, James,2006, "Research methods knowledge base", Cengage Learning
- Turner, J.R, Zolin, R and Remington, K, October, 2009, "Modeling Success on Complex Projects: Multiple Perspectives over Multiple Time Frames", Proceedings of IRNOP IX, Berlin.
- Vierimaa, M, Tihinen, M, Kurvinen, T, May 2001, "Comprehensive approach to software measurement", Proc. of the 4th European Conference on Software Measurement and ICT Control, FESMA-DASMA 2001, Heidelberg, Germany, pp 237-246.
- Vandevoorde, S and Vanhoucke, M, 2006, "A comparison of different Project Duration Forecasting Methods using Earned Value Metrics", International Journal of Project Management.
- Wang, YingXu, 2003, "The Measurement Theory for Software Engineering", IEEE CCECE, pp 1321 - 1324 vol.2.
- Wilkens, Tammo T, 1999, "Earned Value, Clear and Simple", http://www.acq.osd.mil/pm/old/paperpres/wilkins_art.pdf
- Woody, Carol, March 2005, "Eliciting and Analyzing Quality Requirements: Management Influences on Software Quality Requirements", Technical Note CMU/SEI-2005-TN-010

- Wohlin Claes et al, 2000, Experimentation in Software Engineering, 2000, Kluwer Academic Publishers Norwell.
- Yin, Robert K, 2009, "Case Study Research: Design and Methods", Fourth Edition, SAGE Publications, California.